ISBN 978-0-483-13053-1
PIBN 10178147

CONTENTS

A BRIEF CHRONICLE
OF THE INSTALLATION OF
CHANCELLOR BROWN

BY THE OFFICIAL CHRONICLER, PROFESSOR E. G. SIHLER, PH.D.

In recording the academic events of November 9th and 10th, 1911, the writer almost instinctively feels in himself the attitude of a Janus and of the Janus face: looking both backward and forward. It was not long after the generosity of the late John Stewart Kennedy had made University Heights, with its superb site, its noble library and its large hopes, free of debt that Chancellor H. M. MacCracken laid down his burden. This service was begun not many years after the half century milestone of New York University had been passed, and lasted in all a little more than a quarter-century. He came soon after the crisis of 1881; and after one decade of service, in 1894 he removed the College and the School of Applied Science to University Heights, being a pathfinder, nay a pathmaker, into the newer and stronger life of New York University. During the one year of Interregnum, 1910-1911, the current administration of the University's affairs was entrusted to the Syndic of the University, Dr. J. H. MacCracken, and that year of service was marked by the issuance of a report which exhibited with admirable lucidity the financial status of the corporation as well as the literary and professional productivity of the academic teachers during the preceding half decade.

In the latter part of April, 1911, the friends as well as the intraparietal workers of New York University heard with profound interest and steadily increasing acceptance that the Committee of the Corporation had chosen Dr. Elmer Ellsworth Brown, the United States Commissioner of Education at Washington, to be the seventh Chancellor of New York University. As a matter of historical truth, he might be called the second one who almost from the beginning had been devoted to education exclusively, and, if the matter were pressed, the first one of all the seven who had labored himself in *all* the grades of education from the elementary work of the common schools to the work of the Theory of Teaching in two of our foremost State universities (Michigan and California), the whole being crowned by five years of service at the head of the National Bureau of Education at Washington.

The preparations for the installation had been carried on for some time and with a concerted effort of many heads and hearts. In fact, the present historian, whose concerns have extended to the full life of the eighty years of our New York University, from 1830 and 1831 on, recalled no academic occasion whatever in that large period of time, either where the Alumni took so large and vigorous a part, or one which, through the participation of so large and so distinguished a number of our foremost institutions of learning wore and possessed so decidedly a quasi-national air of importance and interest. It seemed as if a universal activity had seized both Corporation and Alumni, and one was reminded of the noble words of a European poet:

> "And in onward, joyous movement
> All the forces stand revealed."

And where so many worked with willing devotion, it would be virtually impossible to name them even, but the initiative and the generous spirit of William M. Kingsley, Esq., A.B., 1883, Treasurer of the corporation, should be especially recorded. Especial reference should also be made to the untiring efforts of the Director of Ceremonies, Edward Hagaman Hall, L.H.M., L.H.D., who arranged many of the features of the program and who was the author of the form used in the Ceremony of the Induction.

On Monday night, November 6th, the gymnasium, draped and adorned as never before in the prevailing tints of the Violet, saw a reception and ball by the undergraduates of University Heights in honor of the Chancellor and Mrs. Brown.

The enumeration of delegates and institutions of learning represented by them will be found further on. Some one hundred and twenty institutions of learning were represented, also the more recent foundations for scientific, academic and social beneficence bearing the names of Mr. Andrew Carnegie, of Mr. John D. Rockefeller and Mrs. Russell Sage. Of this imposing number only the following American institutions antedated 1831, the year in which New York University received its charter, viz.: Bowdoin, University of Vermont, Middlebury, Brown, Yale, Trinity, Harvard, Amherst, Williams, Columbia, Union, Hamilton, the University of the State of New York (as an administrative corporation representing the State directly), the University of

Pennsylvania, Princeton, Hampden-Sidney, and the University of Virginia. The latter was founded by Thomas Jefferson, while his Secretary of the Treasury, Albert Gallatin, was for a short time, and at the beginning, the President of the Council of New York University. The second President of the same, Morgan Lewis, a former Governor of the State of New York, had often slept in the tent of George Washington as the latter's adjutant.

The procession of these one hundred and thirty delegates, in the official garb of academic robes, was given particular distinction by the bright scarlet of Oxford worn by the Right Honorable James Bryce, British Ambassador, whose services to the better self-knowledge of America have been and will be so beneficial, and by the personal presence and share in the exercises on the part of Mr. Andrew Carnegie, whose academic benefactions are known of all men. The exercises of the morning were felicitous in the symbolic functions attending the induction of the new Chancellor: the Secretary of the corporation presenting the great seal; the Librarian of the Law School, the charter; the Bursar of the University offering the keys, and the Senior Professor in actual service, the Hon. Justice Isaac Franklin Russell, bearing a massive silver torch especially presented to New York University by Miss Helen Miller Gould, to whom University Heights and all of New York University is indebted for so great a part of its life and substance. The addresses of both forenoon and afternoon, as well as those at the banquet at the Hotel Astor, will be found in the body of this publication. That the inaugural address of Chancellor Brown must needs claim the largest share of attention for this brief historical notice, goes without saying. It is printed further on, but, even so, it has appeared wise to me to excerpt from it some aphorisms or other important passages. He quoted in modest self-depreciation a phrase from St. Paul: "I am, indeed, in the position of a wild olive which has been graffed into this good olive tree."—"The first requirement of the University's organized research is the requirement, that it shall know the social fabric of which it forms a part."—"Even in our day, when the concentration of educational practice has proceeded much further than in the second quarter of the nineteenth century, our higher education is still largely on an individualistic and competitive basis. Our university spirit is still too largely the spirit of the clan."—"Here is a world within municipal boundaries which is to be a light to itself and to the greater world beyond."—"The occasional outcry against the higher schools can no more check this progress than would a protest against Orion and the sweet influences of Pleiades."—"Yet no one who has apprehended the germinal power of religion in human life can doubt that through all manner of change, and even through occasional estrangement, these two are destined to work together to the end." —"It is a matter of wonder that the University should have been able to maintain so good a teaching standard on so small an outlay for instructors."

The large banquet hall of the Hotel Astor was the scene of the Evening Reunion of Guests, Faculties and Alumni. Whether viewed socially or academically, it will stand out and stand by itself as quite the most impressive function in the eighty years of the life of New York University. It also is notable for the cordial felicitations uttered directly to Chancellor Brown by a delegate from Harvard, and by the Presidents of Yale, of Columbia, a delegate from Princeton (at this moment still without a president) and the President of Cornell. Canada had spoken in the afternoon through a distinguished jurist, whose solidity of attainments was deepened by his strong grasp of the classics. Ladies added much grace and brightness to the vast assemblage. As to the Alumni, this great day was favored as none other had been; for in the morning the Rev. Dr. Henry Bond Elliot of the class of 1840 had spoken, spoken with a clear and resonant voice. Even to see and hear a man *who had seen all the Chancellors* who guided our College and its history during so great a part of a century was a rare pleasure. It was as if History herself and Time had taken human form and come before us. Medicine, Law, Graduate School, Pedagogy, Veterinary School, School of Commerce, Accounts and Finance, and especially the "Uptown Schools" were represented in the vast assemblage. In this brief survey we must be content to mention, like some academic vintage of many years, the mere figures of graduation dates: '40, '43, '47, '48, '54, '56, '60, '62, '63, '65, '69, '71, '72, '74, '75, '76, '78, '80, '82, and all succeeding classes. In fact, every interest was there, and everything was pulsating with joy and hope and beaming such sentiments from happy faces.

The exercises of the second day, Friday, November 10th, were held in the Auditorium at University Heights. Chancellor Brown presided. It was a convocation for educational discussion, details of which will be published in a later bulletin. The themes assigned were largely concerned with the problems and functions of an urban university. The idea of this discussion was a distant result of the very first general conference on the problems of higher education ever held in the United States. It was the so-called "Convocation of Literary and Scientific Gentlemen, held in the Common Council Chamber of the City of New York, October, 1830." It was in the era of John Quincy Adams and Andrew Jackson. That this important conference had its discussions duly recorded was largely owing to Mr. John Delafield. Many of the names of the participants have not lost any luster after eighty-one years. There were present Hodge and Patton of Princeton, Silliman and H. E. Dwight of Yale, Jared Sparks, Theodore Woolsey, Francis Lieber, John Trumbull, Dr. Emory, Gallaudet and Albert Gallatin. Letters were received from Judge Story, from Edward Everett and from George Bancroft.

After eighty-one years another convocation was held; apart from many professors of New York University, the following institutions were represented: Harvard, Columbia, Union College, Brown, Vanderbilt, The Chautauqua Institution, The Polytechnic Institute of Brooklyn, Wells College, Oberlin College, University of Vermont, the University of (the State of) Washington, Fordham University, the Normal College of the City of New York, Ohio State University, Haverford College, the College of the City of New York, the Institute and Training School of Young Men's Christian Associations, Chicago, Ill. Dr. Henry Leipziger, the enthusiastic organizer and Director of the Lectures for the People, took an important part in the discussions of the afternoon.

THE MORNING EXERCISES

The morning exercises opened with an academic procession of more than 700 persons across the Campus, through the Hall of Fame, down Morse Walk to the Mall and thence into the Library. The procession was made up of four divisions. The first division consisted of the speakers, led by Honorary Marshal Edward E. McCall, LL.D., '84' Justice of the Supreme Court and President of the Alumni Association of the Law School, and the Governing Bodies and Patrons of the University, led by Honorary Marshal Gerard B. Townsend, B.S., LL.B., '87' The second division consisted of the Delegates from Foreign Institutions, with DeWitt L. Pelton, Ph.D., '85 as Honorary

Marshal, the Delegates from Institutions in the United States, led by Honorary Marshal Victor J. Dowling, LL.D., '90, Justice of the Supreme Court, and the National State and City Officials led by Honorary Marshall Ernest Hall, LL.D., '66, Ex-Justice of the Supreme Court. The third division included the faculties of the ten university schools marching in the order of the foundation of schools. The fourth Division consisted of the Honorary Alumni and Alumnae, the Alumni of Arts and Sciences and the Representatives of Classes of the University Schools, the Honorary Marshal of this division being David H. Ray, Sc.D., '02, Chief Engineer, Bureau of Buildings of the City of New York. As the head of the procession reached the library porch, the columns divided while a countermarch was executed, the rear of the procession marching first into the library, the speakers entering last.

The presiding officer of the morning exercises was Dr. George Alexander, President of the University Council. The Invocation was given by Dr. Francis Brown, President of Union Theological Seminary. After a rendition of Handel's Largo by the organ and orchestra the chairman called upon Eugene Stevenson, Vice-President of the Council, for the first address of the morning.

ADDRESS ON BEHALF OF THE CORPORATION

"Mr. President, Ladies and Gentlemen: A pleasant and easy task has been assigned to me to-day. As the representative of the Corporation of New York University I am to greet you and bid you welcome, and this I do with all my heart. And then I am to tell you in a few words, what probably you all know already, why we are assembled here.

We meet to inaugurate the seventh Chancellor of our University. Through eighty years of persistent and grinding toil this institution of learning has attained its present place of usefulness and power. The world at large will never know the stories of poverty, labor and self-sacrifice which are written with a pen of iron in our unread and unpublished chronicles.

To-day the clouds have lifted and the sky is bright, and it may be (who knows?) that the immortal spirits of Frelinghuysen, Ferris, Draper, Martin, Mott and Pomeroy, and all their faithful associates in their work of love are with us now, sharing our joy and hope, and giving us their tender, solemn benediction.

We have had strong men to guide us in the past from Frelinghuysen to MacCracken. The achievements of the grand old man who has just laid down the burden of leadership will be written large in the history of New York University. But we live in the present, and to-day our eyes are turned upon the future.

> 'Time is like a fashionable host,
> That slightly shakes his parting guest by the hand;
> And with his arms outstretch'd, as he would fly,
> Grasps in the comer.'

The coming man whom we grasp in our arms, the present Chancellor of New York University, is with us here to-day to be installed in the place of responsibility and power which he will occupy, we hope, for many, many years.

The Corporation of the University with pride and confidence presents Elmer Ellsworth Brown as its Chancellor to its faculties, its students, its alumni, and to the great intellectual, social and religious world which is represented in the life of this great city.

May I say in conclusion one word to the great loyal body of alumni of the University in all its departments. Give, I beg you, to the man whom we have chosen as your leader, your trust, your affection, your enthusiastic support. Fellow alumni present here to-day, I boldly and urgently ask and claim on behalf of the University Corporation, that you at all times hold up the hands of Chancellor Brown, stand by him, and especially try to cheer his heart in every hour of discouragement with the consciousness of your loving sympathy.

The springs of life and usefulness of New York University must rise from the lives and hearts and service of her children. If you and I, all the grateful sons and daughters of our Alma Mater, will give her and her new leader trustful and sympathetic support, the future history of New York University will be a record only of splendid and successful effort—of noble and lasting achievement—in that wide and beautiful field where men work for mankind."

THE LETTER OF APPOINTMENT

The presiding officer called upon George A. Strong, Secretary of the Council, for the reading of the letter of appointment.

April 24, 1911.

ELMER ELLSWORTH BROWN, Ph.D., LL.D.,
  United States Commissioner of Education,
  WASHINGTON, D. C.

DEAR SIR:

I have the honor to inform you that at a meeting of the Council of New York University, held April 24, 1911, you were unanimously elected to be Chancellor of the University, to succeed Henry Mitchell MacCracken, D.D., LL.D., whose resignation, accepted with sincere regret, took effect upon his seventieth birthday anniversary on the 28th of September last.

In calling you to the office so brilliantly and successfully filled by one who, as Vice-Chancellor and Chancellor during a quarter of a century, has done so much to raise the University to its present distinguished position among the educational institutions of our Country, we feel confident that his mantle will fall upon capable shoulders.

Your own successful career as teacher and administrator, covering a period of thirty years, beginning in the public schools of the west, continuing in two of our well-known American universities, and for the last five years in the office of United States Commissioner of Education, has qualified you, we believe, to carry forward effectively the work of New York University, and to make you a worthy successor to your six predecessors in the Chancellorship.

If it shall please you to accept this election, we shall be happy to have you enter upon the discharge of your duties on the 1st day of July next, and we will arrange for your public installation at some convenient date in the fall.

Trusting that this invitation to a large field of usefulness in the Metropolis will appeal to you as a call to duty and will evoke your early acceptance, I remain, in behalf of the Council of the University, with assurances of our high esteem,

Yours very truly,

GEORGE A. STRONG,
  *Secretary of the Council
  of New York University.*

HE HALL OF FAME

MacCracken; Vice-President Stevenson;
ng of the University Council; Professor

Fron

THE INDUCTION

After the reading of the letter of appointment the audience was requested to stand while the ceremony of Induction was performed. The Librarian of the Law School bearing the Charter and Statutes, the Secretary of the Council bearing the Great Seal, the Bursar bearing the Keys and the Senior Professor bearing the Torch, came forward and took their stand near the President of the Council, who spoke as follows:

"ELMER ELLSWORTH BROWN, Doctor of Philosophy and Doctor of Laws, the Council of New York University, exercising the authority vested in it by its Charter and Statutes, and reposing confidence in your character and ability, has elected you to the high and responsible office of Chancellor of the University, and has now summoned you to this presence, to the end that you may, before the Council and these witnesses, reaffirm your consent heretofore given and receive public confirmation of your authority.

It is my duty, in behalf of the Council, representing the Government and Estate of the University, to charge you that you assume this office with firm resolution to devote your powers single-heartedly to the upbuilding of the University and to the moral and intellectual edification of those who enter within its gates.

As Chancellor, you become the Executive Head of the University. As the Chairman of the Executive Committee, as a member of every Standing Committee, as the Head of each Faculty, as the medium of communication between each Faculty and the Council and between the Students and the Council, as the Supervisor of the performance of the work entrusted to subordinate officers and to those instructing the youth who enter these doors, your influence, as Counsellor and Friend, Leader and Helper, touches every part of the University's life. And when, in the fullness of time, the impress of this University has been stamped upon the character of its students, it is your hand that bestows upon the graduates those outward testimonials and honors which alike betoken the privileges which they have enjoyed and stamp the seal of approval upon the work which the University has wrought in them.

Seeing then the sacred nature of these duties, I ask of you, in the name of the Council of the University, do you remain steadfast in your purpose to assume these weighty responsibilities, and do you in the presence of these witnesses ratify your consent to take upon you this office?"

CHANCELLOR-ELECT: "I do."

PRESIDENT OF THE COUNCIL: "Will you perform these duties in the spirit of sacrificing service to your fellow-men putting away all self-seeking, and looking for the recompense of a good conscience and the knowledge of a high steward-ship well and faithfully discharged?"

CHANCELLOR-ELECT: "I will, by God's help."

PRESIDENT OF THE COUNCIL: "Then by the power dele-gated to me by the Council, I confirm you in the office of the Chancellor of the University, and confer upon you all the authority, rights, honors and insignia to that office pertain-ing:"

DELIVERY OF CHARTER AND STATUTES

"And that you may have a continuing remembrance of the high authority of this University as a part of the educa-tional system of the State and of your privileges and responsibilities derived therefrom, I deliver to you a copy of the Charter granted by the State of New York and of the Statutes of the University made pursuant thereto, fervently praying that your labors may be richly fruitful in cultivating the objects for which the University was in-corporated." (Here the Librarian of the Law School came forward and delivered to the Chancellor the Charter and Statutes of the University.)

DELIVERY OF GREAT SEAL

"That you may know the sign by which, together with your signature, the official acts of the University are to be attested, I deliver to you the Great Seal of the University. As this sign encourages, with the motto *"Perstare et Praestare,"* those who run in the uplifted light, so may your administration, in its impress upon those who here seek the prizes of wisdom and knowledge, inspire them, in their life course, to persist and excel in all that is good, and noble, and true of heart." (Here the Secretary of the Council came forward and delivered to the Chancellor the Great Seal of the University.)

DELIVERY OF KEYS

"As a token of your jurisdiction over the material fabric of the University, and a reminder that your manifold duties relate as well to its corporal growth as to its educational efficiency, I deliver to you the Keys of the University. May you so conserve the interests committed to your care that the University shall stand well-approved in the sight of men, and shall merit that support which is requisite for its maintenance." (Here the Bursar came forward and delivered to the Chancellor the Keys of the University.)

DELIVERY OF TORCH

"But that you may not forget that the chief function of this Institution, the very reason for its being, is to enlighten the minds and kindle the aspirations of those who enter its precincts, I deliver to you this Torch as a symbol of your ministry to the informing spirit of the University. Under your guidance, may it continue to shine as a light set upon a hill, illuminating with true knowledge the minds of those who approach its sacred flame." (Here the Senior Professor came forward and delivered the Torch to the Chancellor.)

The President of the Council then turned to the assembly of witnesses and said:

"FORASMUCH as Elmer Ellsworth Brown, Doctor of Philosophy and Doctor of Laws, having been elected Chancellor of New York University, has accepted his election and promised faithfully to discharge the duties of that office, and has been duly invested with all the dignity, powers, privileges and insignia of Chancellor of the University, I require that all persons subordinate to the authority of the Chancellor yield him obedience as such. We crave for him and for the University the friendly support and sympathetic co-operation of the great community here represented, to the end that the University may fulfill to the utmost its functions as an instrument of human culture. And that it may be a power for the enlightenment and uplift of mankind, whose beneficent influence may grow from generation unto generation, we invoke upon the relation now established the favor of Almighty God."

THE INAUGURAL ADDRESS

The audience having taken their seats the presiding officer introduced Elmer Ellsworth Brown, Seventh Chancellor of the University, who gave the following address:

"It is fitting that one who assumes this high responsibility should pay his tribute of respect to the Fathers of the University and declare his adherence to the principles which they builded into its foundation. Such a declaration would seem peculiarly appropriate when the incoming chancellor, as in the present instance, was not born into the family of

New York University, but has been adopted from the outer world.

I am, indeed, in the position of a wild olive which has been graffed into this good olive tree.   The outer world from whence I have come is that of educational institutions under governmental control, of which the most advanced scholastic representatives are the western state universities. Must that earlier allegiance then be forsworn in entering upon these newer relations? After many years of service in the Universities of Michigan and California, which I have come to hold in deep reverence and affection, such a severance of the old ties would not only be personally painful: it might seem to indicate a certain lack of academic principles and loyalty on the part of him who should make the change.

Let it be said, then, at the outset, that the reason why a man may come with so great freedom into New York University from the state universities of the West, is that he may bring his convictions with him.   The essential spirit of those universities has been conspicuously present in this institution from the beginning.   Both its earlier and its later history, indeed, is full of that sense of public duty and responsibility which has gained for the state universities their present influence and leadership.   These institutions are alike in interpreting their public obligation as an obligation to the whole people.   It is not too much to say that some of the earliest and clearest utterances setting forth this more modern conception of academic service, were those which accompanied the founding of the University of the City of New York.

The institution was to be established 'on a liberal foundation, which shall correspond with the spirit and wants of our age and country, which shall be commensurate with our great and growing population, and which shall enlarge the opportunities of education.' It was proposed at the very beginning that ample provision should be made for the customary classical and professional education; but that there should be added thereto an opportunity for training for agricultural, commercial, and the higher mechanical pursuits, together with other provision for other needs which the scholastic tradition had failed to meet.

The most advanced ideal of our state universities has been set forth by President Van Hise, of the University of Wisconsin, who has said of that institution that it proposes to render to the state every needed educational service for which it shall be found the fittest instrument. It would be hardly more than the reiteration of a fundamental principle of New York University to say that this foundation proposes to be as widely serviceable as possible in the higher education of this community, in so far as it shall be found a fit instrument for such service.

1. An institution which is committed to the program of doing new things to meet new conditions, is committed thereby to a new study from time to time of the situation in which its part is to be played. The first requirement of the University's organized research is the requirement that it shall know the social fabric of which it forms a part. In other words, the first business of a modern urban university, such as this, is to know the life and needs of the modern city which it serves. The study of the city's life and needs from this point of view, is not to be an occasional undertaking, but a continuous activity, an indispensable part of the University's system of research and of administration.

But since to know thoroughly is to interpret, it is not enough that the city's life and industry be the subject of continual study in university departments of economics, of statistics, and of sociology: the University is to have insight into the forces which make for betterment, into the striving after civic righteousness, into that pride in all things honorable and beautiful which makes the city desirable as a place where men may live the one, true life of man. The University is to know these things as a participant and a creator. In the spiritual world demand and supply are subtly joined together. The supply precedes and creates the demand. The University is to be to the city a maker of new and higher wants. It is to offer that which men, having seen, shall desire with the purest striving of the human spirit.

2. Let it not be thought, however, that this University or any university can limit itself to merely local relationships. New York University from the beginning was designed to render its first service to the City of New York. Yet it was from the beginning, by statutory provisions, a member of the University of the State of New York. Furthermore, in the very nature of our social organization, this University and every university in all the land, is a participant in our national scheme of higher education. It becomes in reality a member of our National University. The Fathers of New York University saw this truth, even in

their day of educational separatism and isolation; and they gave expression to their faith by calling a convention of the leaders of collegiate education in their own and in other states. Even in our day, when the concentration of educational practice has proceeded much further than in the second quarter of the nineteenth century, our higher education is still largely on an individualistic and a competitive basis. Our university spirit is still too largely the spirit of the clan. In this respect, universities lag behind the better spirit of the age. The conception of a national education, in which every institution is an organ of one comprehensive organism, and all are members one of another—this conception is gaining ground but slowly. Nevertheless, it is gaining ground, and our higher patriotism is bound up with it.

This institution holds itself to be an essential part of the Nation's University. So far as in it lies, it will labor for the building up of our national education. It will live and do its appointed work for all of our people, throughout the land. It will look for an attendance of students from all of our states; and in an important sense it will endeavor to be a true intermediary between the life of the city and the life of the country at large.

But even while we are considering our relations with education conceived as a national concern, we find that the national view itself has become too narrow. There have already appeared the beginnings of an international and even a world system of higher education. A world-standard of academic teaching and academic degrees is almost insensibly taking form and gaining recognition. No true university can be indifferent to this situation. No university can hold the unqualified regard and confidence of its students and its benefactors unless it make for itself a genuinely international character. It must assure to its graduates an unquestioned standing in the world of scholarship. And it must enter without disparagement into those common labors through which all true universties are determining what the world standards in education shall be. This is an historic condition, but it takes new form and significance in our modern age.

That this institution has long been mindful of an ecumenical character which attaches to the university name, has been made evident in many ways: by the goodly number of students from foreign countries to whom it has given instruction, by the wide distribution of the publications of its most eminent teachers, and notably in recent time by visits

THE HEAD OF THE MORNING PROCESSION ENTERING THE LIBRARY

of its Chancellor Emeritus to the universities of the Scandinavian countries and of other parts of the world for the promotion of a mutual understanding among the scholars and teachers of these lands.

From the widest reach of academic relationships, however, we come back to the questions which lie at our door. The more we contemplate the scholastic solidarity of the civilized world, the more clearly we shall apprehend the educational problem of our own metropolitan area. Here is a world within municipal boundaries. Its people in great numbers are entering the higher schools. Even so it is far behind other cities and even behind whole states in the proportion which the attendance upon its colleges and universities bears to its total population. Ohio, with a population equal to that of this city, has 3,000 more students in its higher institutions. Twenty other states show a larger proportionate attendance. Chicago, Philadelphia, and the metropolitan district of Boston, the three cities next in size to New York, all show a higher attendance ratio. If New York came up even to the average of these three cities, the attendance upon her colleges and universities would aggregate not 12,000 students, as at the present time, but not far from 20,000 students.

These figures are cited neither for praise nor for blame. They admit of a variety of explanation. The moral which they point in our present discussion is simply this, that New York is not now sending an over-large fraction of its population to college; that it is, in fact, educating only a very moderate proportion of its people in its higher institutions; and that it will in all probability show a great increase in its college attendance within the coming years. The normal increase of over 100,000 souls a year in its population, and still more the general advance of a civilization which is peculiarly dependent upon the agencies of instruction: these things point to a great expansion of collegiate attendance within the immediate future. Be sure that our institutions of learning will be taxed to the utmost to accommodate those who will flock to them for instruction. The occasional outcry against the higher schools can no more check this progress than would a protest against Orion and the sweet influences of Pleiades.

Not only as regards collegiate instruction, but as regards science and the arts, the city will make increasing demand upon the universities, and the universities will render to the city an increasing service. Public administration is gradually growing more scientific. The problems of public health and sanitation, of the supply of pure food and pure water, of transportation and related public services, of taxation, of uniform and consistent legislation, of parks and playgrounds, of landscape architecture and other arts in their public applications—all of these things are already making demands for expert knowledge and competent investigation. If we add business administration, the organization of industrial undertakings, the study of commercial relations, domestic and foreign, we have fairly begun—but no more than fairly begun—to suggest the growing need to be met in such a city as ours by the higher institutions of learning.

A number of colleges and universities are sharing the burden of this mighty responsibility. I am not unmindful of still other institutions, with large and increasing influence, when I speak at this time particularly of those two which are most frequently mentioned along with New York University, her elder sister, Columbia, and her junior, the City College. In an especial sense, it would seem incumbent upon these three institutions that they confer from time to time regarding the general interests of higher education in the City of New York, and that they devise ways in which the educational needs of our metropolitan people may be more fully met. Their separate autonomy and their individual character and mission may not for a moment be called in question. But it is not unlikely that these three, and other institutions working with them, may through concerted action add much to the educational advantages of this great city. I am confident that New York University will be found ready to do her part in the furtherance of such cooperation.

The vision which comes before us is that of a city, one of the greatest of modern times, and the commercial capitol of our Nation. We look to see it adequately equipped with schools of the higher learning in all branches of human thought and endeavor; and to see these schools and other centers of the spiritual life taking counsel together and taking knowledge of the city's need, till the highest opportunity for education shall be brought within the reach of all of our citizens, according to their ambition and their native abilities; while science and the arts shall find their widest application in the city's life. We look, moreover, to see those united agencies of instruction each year scrutinizing anew the city's life and destiny, and going on before its advance, with new plans for better achievements; till the people, being enlightened at home beyond the common experience of man, shall have light to spread abroad wherever their name and their commerce shall run.

3. Before we go further with considerations relating particularly to New York University, let us consider with the utmost brevity, some of the essential characteristics of any university. Public service is good, but "The gift without the giver is bare." What, then, is a true university, which is to render these public services?

The ancient world furnishes one answer, which is fundamental and cannot be set aside. A university is an institution for the cultivation of the good, the true, and the beautiful. Its relation to the true is universally recognized, at least the true in the typical forms of the physical and mathematical sciences. To put men in possession, not only of well-grounded scientific knowledge, but of the methods by which such knowledge is acquired and extended, to put men in possession of those standards of precision and of fidelity to fact which characterize the scientific spirit— these things are the very elements and commonplaces of university instruction. The freedom of science is the foundation stone of a university. The university man is the scientific man.

But the beautiful is equally an essential object of university cultivation, and science requires the association with art to come to its best. So art requires association with science to come to its best. Of these two, each corrects a certain immaturity and intolerance in the other. Accordingly the alliance of the fine arts with the universities, which has had a fluctuating and uncertain history, is by all means to be fostered and encouraged, along with the alliance of the universities with the physical and the philosophical sciences.

This double alliance with the beautiful and the true is imperative, moreover, if universities are to cultivate adequately the good. So far as the moral life is concerned, universities do not seek merely to intensify ethical sentiments, but to link them most intimately with an organic system of ideas. Your true university man is one whose moral emotions are buttressed and reinforced by knowledge and good taste.

In its thought concerning the good, the ancient world rose to a height which transcended the Greek conceptions, and gave to mankind the elements of religion. The modern world, in a thousand ways, has readjusted the relations of

religion and education to each other. Such readjustments
will undoubtedly go forward in the future. Yet no one who
has apprehended the germinal power of religion in human
life can doubt that through all manner of change, and even
through occasional estrangement, these two are destined to
work together to the end. The hope for good relations
between religion and education is increased when science
and art are both of them fairly represented, side by side,
in our educational organization.

These venerable conceptions are everlastingly true; but
they must be applied to changing social conditions. Our
modern life finds its all-absorbing problem in the endeavor
to realize a true democracy. Academic institutions are not
now concerned simply with the making of superior men.
They must send out men who are both superior and com-
panionable. The leaders whom they train must be able
to lead, not condescendingly, but through wide co-operation.

It is hard to achieve this combination of democracy with
the leadership of the Best, but in that union lies the very
heart and focus of our modern life. And universities must
succeed in this or yield their place in the van of the world to
some worthier type of institution.

One other combination of diverse elements must be a
constant concern of university instruction. That is the
combination of liberal with vocational instruction, and of
both of these with the cultivation of the peculiar endowment
of individual students. A liberal education fits a man to
view the interests of mankind as if they were his own, while
his vocational training fits him to do his own proper
work as if it were a work for all. The real university
problem here is not the problem of the one or the other of
these forms of education but of their connection one with
another. The effective correlation of a college of liberal arts
and a graduate school with schools of the several professions, is calling for fresh attention to-day, after all of the
working adjustments of the past.

Along with this question, the further problem of the con-
servation of all valuable personal initiative and individuality
is not to be forgotten. A futile and disappointing thing
unless it be deeply grounded, when originality of thought
and character is joined to sound culture and professional
competence, it becomes one of the most precious things in
the world, a thing to be cherished by universities in the
interest of both democracy and leadership.

These are meager lines with which to indicate the character of a true university, but they may serve the present purpose. Some part of such a sketch is well illustrated in the character and career of Samuel F. B. Morse, whose name is inseparably linked with the earlier history of this University. The service, altogether his own, which was rendered by Professor Morse to all humanity, has shed a peculiar luster upon the institution in which he taught the arts and practiced the sciences. It is well that he should be its first representative in that Hall of Fame which New York University holds in trust for the people of the United States. May we cherish the spirit of invention in both science and the arts, along with a continued insistence upon a training broad enough and sufficiently well balanced to furnish the groundwork for invention of the highest order. So may we hope that great public services may continue to come forth from these halls, which shall fire succeeding generations of students to generous emulation.

4. This University now has its existence at four centers, three of them on Manhattan and one in the Borough of the Bronx, and in twelve colleges and other scholastic divisions. While such dispersion has its disadvantages, it seems inevitable in an institution proposing the wide range of educational service on which this University has entered. If its work can be carried on at so many points simultaneously, it would seem that the number might be increased as the need may arise, up to the limit of administrative efficiency. But new work should not be undertaken until there is reasonable assurance that it will receive adequate support. It is particularly difficult to maintain educational standards in any university division for which only an uncertain and insufficient financial provision has been made. To carry out in New York City a program comparable with that of the state universities, would call for even more liberal support than the state universities receive.

Each addition, moreover, must accentuate the necessity of vigorous co-ordination of the several parts. It is clear that the College of Arts and Pure Science is the natural center of the whole system. It should be not only a unifying center but an invigorating center as well. All pains should accordingly be taken to maintain and to advance the academic life at University Heights. Here, on our forty-acre farm, we may have a country college in the heart of a great city. If we shall maintain here a college that is educationally sound and that offers distinctive values, suited to its location and history, then we shall see ambitious students coming to us in increasing numbers; then we shall help city and country to see one another more truly on the high ground of academic vision. The lines of connection, too, between the college and the other University divisions should be strengthened as far as possible.

In a great work of art there are unities which, though not obtrusive, are none the less dominant. In an architectural group, for example, as in the buildings of the World's Fair at Chicago, the uniform height of the cornice lines has served to hold the entire composition firmly in one, while allowing wide diversity in the several parts. A great musical work shows even finer unities in theme and form of composition. The suggested comparison is only a partial indication of the educational organization of which a great university such as this is susceptible—an organization which leaves room for self-government and individuality in the several parts while assuring a positive character to the educational undertaking as a whole. Such an organization, making for freedom rather than for mere subordination, can be achieved only by the several faculties, working in unison. As New York University now stands, the first work of coordination will not have to be done. The ground plan of a complete university organization has been marked out with a firm hand. It is doubtless owing in large measure to this foresight that the way now seems so clear to the next steps in the organizing process.

The freedom and responsibility of the faculties in these matters are to be emphasized. It hardly need be said that the chief business of college faculties is education. Yet that saying would seem to carry with it the corollary that their chief study is education. A university whose several faculties should largely concern themselves with the study of the principles and practice of instruction as related to higher schools and colleges, might do a great work, it would appear, in the way of concentrated efficiency and prevention of waste throughout all of its departments. Such a university might well be an example of the best kind of unification, the kind in which there is no end of non-conformity, but intelligent, discriminating, stimulating non-conformity. The unity of the spirit in some such sense as this is a thing to be desired. It is to be hoped and expected that a university which achieves such educational unity, will be sought out by many of the choice young spirits of the age, from all parts of the land and from other lands, as a place where competent guidance may be had to an

THE MORNING PROCESSION—RANKS DIVIDED FOR THE COUNTERMARCH

Left to right: Honorary Marshal E. E. McCall; Chancellor Brown; President Francis Brown; Dean Clarence D. Ashley; Presley D. Stout; Professor Leslie J. Tompkins; Chief Justice Isaac Franklin Russell.

education which is richly worth getting. Such co-operating faculties might impart to a division of liberal arts some of the seriousness of purpose and insistence upon the things that really count, which characterizes the best professional schools; and might impart to a professional division some of that broadly scientific spirit and devotion to public service which is one of the finest flowers of a liberal culture. The two sides, in such a case, would understand each other and really work together.

The School of Pedagogy, in addition to its other golden opportunities, has here a chance to render a noteworthy service. Is it not fair to expect that the systematic study of education, which in such a school is commonly confined to the elementary and secondary grades of instruction, should now and again overflow its banks, and contribute to the making of a pedagogy of the higher education?

By whatever means the end may be accomplished, we cannot doubt that where college faculties are not only effective in teaching but are also expert in dealing with the large problems of education, they will become the true directors of studies to our great classes of university students, who too often waste time through sheer lack of such convincing guidance. It is with large confidence in what the faculties of this University are doing and will do, that I am entering upon a work in the details of which many of their members are more experienced and expert than I. And it is done with a great hope that more and more this may be found to be a good place for the best men to do the work of college instruction.

5. Personal elements and personal values claim particular attention in all of our planning. This University is rich in memories of men and women who, as its students, teachers, governors, friends, and benefactors, have served their age in affectionate loyalty to its name and its ideals. To-day we recall the lives of those who have passed on into larger life; we greet the living who are assembled here, and we send forth our thoughts and our good will to those who are with us in spirit only while they carry on their appointed work in many fields and in many lands. Already, because of the warmth of the greeting which has been extended to me, I find myself identified with the life of the institution in its manifold activities, and abounding in confidence of close relations with those on whom there rests the immediate responsibility for the various university undertakings.

Instruction is an affair of the university, by the faculties, and for the student body. That it may come to its best, the interests of the teaching staff must be carefully guarded. It is a matter of wonder that this University should have been able to maintain so good a teaching standard on so small an outlay for instruction. The situation is one which reflects credit upon the staff of instructors, who in the face of grave difficulty, have shown devotion to their teaching and to the institution of which they are members; and credit also upon the general management of the University, which has carried the courses of instruction forward under circumstances so adverse. Chancellor MacCracken, who had borne for many years the chief burden of this responsibility, and to whom the University is mainly indebted for the mighty transformation of the two decades just past, saw before the close of his administration the dawn of a new day in the finances of the institution. While that day has already dawned, the University is not yet out of the twilight; but there is at least a strong hope and expectation that the improvement of conditions affecting the corps of instruction may go steadily, even if all too slowly, forward.

It is not forgotten that the work of a university is for its students. But the students themselves have so much to do with the shaping of their own affairs, that one is tempted to employ another paraphrase of Lincoln's saying, and declare that a college education is an education of, for, and by students. There are advantages in such a situation. No man is educated until he is self-educated, and we may expect a true light to arise on the problem of college training from those activities which students undertake on their own account. It is the part of simple wisdom that we should maintain an appreciative and indeed a respectful attitude toward those activities.

It does not follow, however, that college faculties are to fall back into an attitude of subordination, after the mediæval precedent of Bologna. From an acquaintance with some few college generations, I am sure that our American students do not ask to be left to their own devices. They do not desire a soft and easy college course. Except for a small percentage—and in New York University I have not yet found even that group—they are ready to go through fire and water for the cause they believe in, and to follow the leaders who can command their confidence. I have no desire to see stiff requirements heaped up by the college, simply because they are severe. But we need have no fear of stiffness and even severity so long as it carries our students forward to a genuine education. The college that follows the policy of educating well at any cost, even at the cost of hardness and toil, is a college they will love to their dying day, and its diploma will be among their dearest possessions. Such a college I believe every one of the Colleges of New York University has striven to be in the past and such I believe they will strive to be in the future. They deeply value the loyalty and affection of their students and their alumni; and they will strive to hold and deepen that devotion, not by any bids for an evanescent popularity, but by incessant occupation with the task of offering an education that shall educate.

The University values its friends, and it seeks a wider circle of friends. You will ask whether I mean friends who will give largely for its support. And I answer, yes. There is no reason why I should hesitate to say that the University needs and desires such friends. Its purpose is so large that any achievement seems small by comparison. It will need an enlarged and enlarging support to do its proper work. There are a score of directions in which help is needed at the present time. I have alluded to the munificent bequest of Mr. John S. Kennedy, which has cleared the educational plant of the University from debt, and made possible a new beginning in its great enterprise. The heightened hope and courage of our several colleges bears witness to the good which this bequest has wrought. In like manner, the earlier gifts of Miss Gould, Mrs. Sage, Mr. Carnegie, Mr. Havemeyer, Mr. Charles Butler, and others whose high and generous liberality has been equally appreciated—these in like manner have from time to time brought new hope and courage to the builders of this University. Their deeds, without which there would be no university here, should receive acknowledgment on such an occasion as this.

But by friends of the University, I do not mean those only who can give into its treasury. Those donors who have made possible its improvement and expansion within the last preceding administration have repeatedly bestowed upon it a gracious personal interest which has multiplied the value of their gifts. We desire that personal interest on the part of those also who cannot offer any material bounty, for it is itself a gift beyond price. We need a wider understanding and appreciation of the large purpose and the high responsibilities of this institution. We need to have it more generally known in the City of New York that this is not the City College, nor even a department of Columbia University. Doubtless both of those institutions will share in this desire. We need friends whose counsel and criticism will be to us as a breath of mountain air, when we come upon our dull and sultry days of doubt and sheer discouragement.

We seek the good-will of our neighbors, of many classes and occupations. An enthusiastic alumnus said the other day, 'Why, New York University can have the good-will of every washerwoman in the Bronx.' I hope it may have that good-will and deserve it. It would be quite in accord with American traditions if from some of those humble homes there should come in the next generation men who should reflect the greatest distinction upon the University and upon the commonwealth. We value our relations with the public schools, and we hope for increasing nearness to those secondary schools, both public and private, from which our students are to come.

We seek the good-will of our sister institutions in this land and in foreign lands, whose written messages and whose greeting by their personal representatives have added so greatly to the interest and the distinction of this assembly. Their co-operation and even their generous rivalry will be tonic, and the sense that we are of one family with them all, will strengthen our hands whenever it is brought to mind.

A great company has gathered at this ceremonial and we are conscious of a greater cloud of witnesses who look down from the 'height beyond the height.' All of the original founders of the University are of that larger company. Of the former chancellors there is left only the latest of the line, who, sitting here with us, can look about him upon a University, every division of which is now a monument to his constructive and reconstructive genius. They have made this University the center of a very religious devotion, and the bearer of the purest fire of our Christian civilization. May their intentions and their hopes be abundantly realized.

God helping me, I will do the part committed to me. And speaking more impersonally—for every man comes to his best success only when his individual service is merged in the larger life of an institution—God helping her, New York University will do the work that is given her to do."

ADDRESSES OF CONGRATULATION

The Inaugural Address was followed by Handel's Hallelujah Chorus by the organ and orchestra. The presiding officer then announced the addresses of congratulation, the first of which was given by Henry Mitchell MacCracken, D.D., LL.D., Chancellor Emeritus.

ADDRESS OF THE CHANCELLOR EMERITUS

"From the administrations that are past I bring congratulations to my successor, as he enters upon the New York University Chancellorship. This official title comprises in its three words three distinct names—'New York,' 'New York University,' 'New York University Chancellorship.' I will say a word as to each. I shall not speak of the past for lack of time, nor of the future—for it doth not yet appear as to any one of these three things what it shall be.

This City of New York is an area of land and water within a boundary of about a hundred miles. It is also a collection of buildings with their contents. If every dollar of the tax appraisal represents one day's work, and it is more likely to stand for two or three days' work, New York is the product in tangible form of thirty millions of years of human lives. Chiefly, New York consists of five millions of souls, or, if we include such part of New Jersey as is nearer to our City Hall than is University Heights, of six millions of souls within less than sixty minutes of the Chancellor's office at Washington Square. Here is all the complexity of a modern community, industrial, financial, intellectual, political, social and spiritual. It is to-day the metropolis of the western continent; prophets say that it will be the metropolis of our earth. Having recently visited every city of the world claiming over a million inhabitants, except the cities of Russia and South America, I return more ready than ever to love and to praise our proud city of the waters.

What is New York University? Legally, a corporation of thirty-two persons of any age over twenty-one, of any race or faith or condition, provided that a fraction of them must be citizens of New York. Pedagogically, it is a composite of eight degree-giving faculties, with one hundred Professors and twice that number of instructors and helpers, who are teaching now as many students as our buildings can hold, and more than they can accommodate. Racially, our corporation and faculties are Americans of mingled bloods,

the Teutonic predominating.   Politically, they are Liberal
rather than Tory, and Tammany as well as Black Republican.   Ecclesiastically, they are broad rather than high,
and Presbyterian more than Catholic.   They belong to that
small minority of universities in this state which have no
legal connection with any church.   Beneficiarily—if I may
coin a word—New York University can count only a half
dozen benefactors who have given gifts that reached six
figures; only one benefactor who used seven figures.   Nine-
tenths, if not ninety-nine-hundredths of the persons who
have cast gifts into our treasury have used only four or
three or even two figures.   I have even fulfilled the official
duty of acknowledging gratefully the gift of a book to
our library, which, if it had been offered at public auction,
would not have brought the widow's two mites which make
a farthing.   The Omniscient only knows what person has
given the most to New York University.

Not a dollar of its property has come from the Government, national or state or municipal.   On the contrary, the
University is urging against the city a claim for a roadway
to the station which was acknowledged by Mayor Low's
administration, approved by Mayor McClellan's, but up to
date has been repudiated by the present fusion administration.   It is also urging a claim against the state, for com-
pensation for injury done by state competition to the oldest
veterinary college in America.   I learn that both the Republican Legislature of 1910, and the Democratic of 1911,
recognized that the State should not crush private business
by state college labor, any more than by state prison labor,
but the Governors Hughes and Dix, by their vetoes, placed
economy before speedy justice.   My successor, who for a
score of years has served Government education, will know
how to urge the just claims of New York University
against both the city and the state.

Private giving has made our University.   The main ob-
stacle in its way for a quarter century has been the epidemic
of business consolidation.   Persons afflicted by this malady
apply rules invented for building up the tobacco business
to the building up of universities.   Under the medical treat-
ment of Dr. Taft and of Congress, this epidemic is abating.
Such a clear intellect as that of the late John S. Kennedy
thought it well to endow university competition in New
York City.

In circling the globe the past year, I was surprised to
be met in at least ten cities of Asia by New York University

Chie Justice Isaac I
rank A. Fall

h;

MORNING PROCESSION—THE DELEGATES ENTERING THE HALL OF FAME

Left to right: Acting Dean Herbert M. Denslow and Professor Charles M. Shepard, representing General Theological Seminary; U. S. Senator Elihu Root, Hamilton College; Professor Benjamin M. Davis, Miami University; Professor James Oscar Boyd, Princeton Theological Seminary; President John Martin Thomas and Dr. Alonzo Barton Hepburn, Middlebury College.

alumni. They represented five of our degree-giving schools. In the capital of Japan, seven Japanese alumni had organized a New York University Association of Eastern Japan. Also in West Japan, I was indebted for a dinner to three of our alumni. At the close of a day and a half of railway travel from Pekin southwesterly to Hankow— the center of the present war in China—we expected to find no lodging save on the mail-boat, which was to carry us near a thousand miles down the Yang-tze River; but on the station platform my hand was grasped by a graduate of our Medical College, who said, 'I am in charge of the medical work here in Boone University, and with my wife have a house on the college campus. You must not lodge to-night on the mail-boat.' We did not.

Daniel Webster, in the Supreme Court at Washington, before Chief Justice Marshall, defending Dartmouth College, exclaimed: 'It is, sir, as I have said, a small college, and yet there are those who love it.' It is quite the expected and natural and proper thing that our little University should be loved by a person like myself—who have given half of my mature life to its service and have seen each of my four children enrolled among its alumni. But my experience in Asia and other lands the past year has led me to feel that, even in unexpected corners of the world, there are those who feel—'It is, sir, as I have said, a small university, and yet there are those who love it.'

The third thing that I was to speak of is the Chancellorship of New York University. The ultimate object of this office was spoken of by me twenty-one months ago in my letter of resignation, as follows: 'The helping of a multitude of earnest students, men and women, to lead more effective lives.' Our statutes give wide scope to the Chancellor in striving for this result. They say: 'The Chancellor shall be the executive head of the University, exercising such supervision and direction as will promote its usefulness and growth.' It reminds one of the General Welfare clause of the United States Constitution. Besides doing everything which the University Statutes appoint him to do, he is to care for the large residuum of necessary work, which is everybody's business and, therefore, likely to be nobody's business, unless the Spirit of the Lord moves some man to discern and to perform the task. So the Spirit of the Lord came upon Gideon, on Jeptha and Samson, quite outside their statutory obligations. It came nineteen hundred years ago upon a nobler man, who justified his work in Galilee by saying: 'The Spirit of the Lord is upon me, because he hath appointed me to tasks which are urgent to be done.'

I congratulate New York University that her seventh chancellor will strive toward high educational ideals, and will conscientiously obey the command—'Six days shalt thou labor and do all thy work.' For the University, the chancellor, the deans, the councilors, the professors and the students I would offer the prayer inscribed in the mosaic work on yonder dome:

'And chiefly Thou, Oh Spirit, that dost prefer
Before all temples the upright heart and pure.
Instruct me, for Thou knowest. What in me is dark,
Illumine: what is low, raise and support.'"

THE ADDRESS OF THE SENIOR DEAN

The address of congratulation on behalf of the faculties was given by the Senior Dean. Clarence Degrand Ashley, J.D., LL.D., of the University School of Law. who spoke as follows:

"On behalf of the several faculties of this University I have the honor and privilege of extending to you a cordial welcome—We tender our sincere greeting.

The broad mind. indomitable will and never failing courage of your predecessor has built up a great institution. After a long struggle, disheartening disappointments, and bitter financial trials, he has brought the University safely to its present position. Upon these broad foundations you are to build further.

To us your office seems pregnant with opportunity. We believe a great future is now before you.

This city is destined to reach an enormous growth— with its material advantages will increase its intellectual demands, and it requires no gift of prophecy to foretell that New York will be a great educational center. The institutions which faithfully and truly meet these demands, which solve the difficult educational problems of the future, will be doing a much needed work for the world.

But these problems require thought and brain. We must all cordially recognize the fact that each university needs and must have the co-operation and aid of its sister institutions. A noble and generous rivalry and emulation spurs to better effort, but any success of one renders the task of the others the easier. Experience abundantly proves this.

The presence here to-day of representatives from our leading collegiate bodies indicates the friendly feeling existing between those engaged in educational work. Here in New York we must not only help each other, but we must also have helpful suggestions from other institutions throughout the world. In our faculties are representatives from all the colleges, some having degrees from two or three of them. The ideals we have thus gained, the lessons of life we have there learned, are now being actively applied by us, and in our turn we are sending out our graduates to help in their work. Each is thus influenced by the ideals of the others.

There is urgent need for all, and there will be ample financial support for all doing worthy work.

For you, Sir, the future offers great promise. Relieved from the daily, harassing financial demands, whch have heretofore beset our executive, you will have more time to devote to the great educational questions of the day. We believe you to be the right man in the right place. We look forward with renewed courage and confidence. We believe that in the far future when you pass on the burden to your successor, the University will have gone through a period of steady, substantial advance, and that you will have carried forward the work most worthily.

We pledge you our hearty co-operation and aid. We greet you with sincere enthusiasm, and again assure you of our earnest sympathy, and deeply felt welcome."

THE ADDRESS OF THE SENIOR CLASS ORATOR

The address of congratulation on behalf of the student-body was given by Presley Downs Stout, Orator of the Senior Class, who spoke as follows:

"Honored Chancellor, Deans and Faculties, Friends, Alumni and Fellow-students of New York University: On this significant occasion, it is my privilege and pleasure to voice the mind of the undergraduate-body. Standing, as we do, at the entrance upon a new stage in our history, we cannot but feel the play of varied sentiments. The presence of him who but recently laid aside the robes of the chief office of our institution recalls the past. Many of us are still undergraduates, who knew and loved him as Chancellor. We are impressed, now as never before, with the magnitude of his work, and the work of those who labored with him; in this work we recognize the solid steps of progress by which we have attained to our present position upon the threshold of a prosperous future; and as we consider the enjoyments which are ours because of his service here, our sense of gratitude and of obligation to push forward that work is profound.

To-day, we bid welcome to a new leader, and our thought is directed toward the future. The outlines of the edifice at whose portal we are standing we may not discern. For that edifice of the future is not yet reared. What its proportions and its beauty shall be, only our use of the time at hand may decide. The building of it is to be our ever-present care. Whether it shall attain to the imposing grandeur of a temple, or but mediocrity of stature, our present hopes, our present counsels, our present efforts, must determine. That is the responsibility of this hour.

The student-body is keenly sensible of its important share in this responsibility. The world estimates the worth of a university by the character of the men who go out from it. That progress of an institution which is indicated in mere wealth of resources and of material equipment would be but an insecure pretence if it had not a firm foundation in the character of the students. The student-body will best promote the interests of our institution as it most persistently strives to maintain a high standard of symmetrical manhood; and will best further the plans of this new administration as it, first of all, endeavors to prove itself worthy to receive the privileges that are being planned for it. Herein lies *our* peculiar obligation and responsibility. Herein is to be found the real criterion of our expressions of loyalty.

We may not see the progress of the future with definite vision. But we may from the present deduce what will indicate its direction. It is not the least significant earnest of the prosperity of this new era that the enthusiasm of our graduate-body and our faculties finds an equal counterpart in the student-body; that already our new leader has won the trust and loyalty of his students. And I am happy to bring to him, together with their congratulation and Godspeed, the confidence, the affection, and the loyal support of the undergraduate-body."

THE ADDRESS OF THE SENIOR ALUMNUS

The address of congratulation on behalf of the Alumni was given by Henry Bond Elliot, A.M., D.D., '40, the Senior Alumnus, who spoke as follows:

"Mr. Chancellor, Ladies and Gentlemen—I appreciate, Mr.

Chairman, the honor of a place on the programme to-day, though it be only to bring up the rear. I am fully aware, however, that I owe it not to eminence of station or ability, such as marks the speakers who have preceded me, but rather to the presence on the Committee of Arrangements of an expert mathematician. When the question of my possible fitness for the position was raised it was referred to him, and he performed a sum in simple addition. He added and he added and he added the years until he was tired and said, 'Oh, well, let him have it, I guess we can stand it, and it will be just this once, give it to him.' They gave it to me and here I am.

I have learned what are some of the incidents and disabilities of age, but I have also learned some of its advantages. People do, somehow, think more of one who has outlived three generations. They give him credit at least for having a good degree of vitality, though they ought rather to give credit to One 'in whose hands our lives are and who has set the bound which we cannot pass.' When, as a boy of fourteen, I paced proudly the halls of the old university building, the gem of the neighborhood, and took my seat in alphabetical order beside a man named Downes, nearly thirty years old, just from the farm, I did not dream that when I should reach my eighty-ninth year I would be called to stand upon this platform, on our noble 'Heights,' to speak in behalf of those who have since passed away. Pardon the egotism. It is only to get a grip upon my subject and to show that I do have a claim upon my place to-day.

It has been my privilege to know all the chancellors. A notable list it is, and from the beginning they have all been progressive. Each in his turn and according to his opportunity has pushed the institution farther on and higher up until it has reached its present status; but of them all, giving due credit to each of them, there is not one who has so far advanced its interests, who has given it such constant, untiring devotion, who has brought it educationally, financially, architecturally and in public estimate, so far as the one who now lays down the office and its burdens. It has really seemed that he must have slept with the university under his pillow, only to take it up again in the morning. Thus, while I greet the incoming chief, I hail the outgoing one.

But I must not forget that I am appointed to speak as the voice of that huge body technically called the 'Alumni,'

and let me add the 'Alumnæ' also. Where shall I find
them that I may speak with authority as their representative? The former and the latter, where are they? They
are. like Israel of old, as 'a nation scattered and peeled.'
Did I say 'peeled'? No! No! No circumstances, whatever
they may be, can strip them of the honors which they have
acquired in all the walks of life. They are of every order
and every faith. Some of them were lineal descendants of
Abraham, the 'Father of the Faithful,' from whom are the
grandest names in history, and who are now some of our
most respected citizens. Others of the lineage of Constan-
tine, lifting high the red banner of the cross, proclaiming
'In this sign we conquer!' They are everywhere. Dr.
MacCracken has just told us how he met them in all the
cities of Asia. He might have found them in the jungles
of Africa, where our missionaries have lived and died. And
everywhere they speak substantially with one voice—one
spirit supremely animates them, the spirit of integrity and
of fealty to obligation. There may be false notes in some
instances, for they are only men, and 'to err is human, to
forgive, divine,' but their discords cannot mar the har-
monies of the whole. Moreover, as fellow-workers in scholastic service, they seek impartially one end. In the history
of our university there has been no aristocracy nor democracy of privileges.. After the manner of the bard of Scotland, we declare that whether with many or with few of the
guineas of rank in these halls 'a mon's a mon for a' that,
and for a' that!' So may it be in the years to come.

I must cease, lest I weary you. What more can I say?
In behalf of this great body, as well as on my own account,
there are two words in which our message of gratulation
can be condensed. The first to you, sir, personally, is 'Welcome.' The other is for ourselves. I speak it reverently.
It is 'Halleluiah!' Amen."

In the absence of Bishop Darlington, the chairman called
from the audience the Rev. Vincent Phraner, D.D., '48
to pronounce the benediction. An adjournment was then
taken until 2:30 P. M. The audience retained their seats
while the procession marched out of the building.

RECESS

Luncheon was served at the gymnasium for the delegates
and honorary guests and in the Psi Upsilon, Zeta Psi, Delta
Phi and Delta Upsilon Fraternity Houses for the alumni
and student representatives.

THE AFTERNOON EXERCISES

At two-thirty o'clock the procession again formed, marched across the campus, through the Hall of Fame and directly into the auditorium. Chancellor Brown as chairman welcomed the representatives as follows:

"We are desirous of having as much time as possible this afternoon to hear from our distinguished guests. So the words of welcome that I will express will take the least possible time, but the shorter they are, the deeper they go.

Let me say to you delegates from institutions of learning in this land and in foreign lands, we welcome you from the bottom of our hearts. We welcome you, Mr. Mayor, and we appreciate your coming to be with us on this occasion. We welcome the friends of the University who are here to-day, representing this and that body, or representing only themselves. We welcome you from the bottom of our hearts.

The first response that is announced on our program comes appropriately from the State of New York, by the Honorable Andrew Sloan Draper, LL.D., State Commissioner of Education."

RESPONSE FOR THE STATE OF NEW YORK

ANDREW S. DRAPER, LL.D., STATE COMMISSIONER OF EDUCATION

"Mr. Chancellor, there are so many people in the State of New York, that it is impossible to collect and compound their sentiments upon any subject not already well settled in American public policy unless it is a matter of practically universal and paramount concern. But the support of all schools, high and low, is among the settled policies, indeed is a confirmed passion in America, and I am sure all the people will be glad to have their interest in these uncommon exercises expressed to this University, and their good wishes presented with warmth of feeling to its new Chancellor.

States are very dependent upon universities, even though all the people do not always appreciate them. It is quite possible that states and universities may wholly misunderstand one another. Scholarship is frequently dazed by politics, and politics is sometimes brutally indifferent to scholarship. On ordinary days it is very hard for them to mix, for scholars have very little patience with the practical difficulties of the state, and the state is not likely to become excited over such questions as whether classical history or scientific research is entitled to the most support; or whether training boys and girls in vocational industries is likely to deprive the professions of medicine and law of the necessary novitiates and prove a menace to the very life of universities. So, the state is glad to come into this University on a day when it will not encounter the danger of running into phantom fights over academic questions which it might not understand.

This is a University with a noble history; it is doing efficient work; and it is looking out upon enticing prospects. It is in a great city where there is no end of people to be trained for every kind of leadership, and no end of every manner of work for universities to do. The state asks it to uphold scholarship and do what it can to apply scholarship to life, and, knowing that such is its aim the state wishes this University well.

It is my great pleasure particularly to felicitate New York University upon the accession of the new Chancellor. He has attributes which appeal very strongly to the people of the state. He was born upon a New York farm. Whether or not it is better to be born upon a farm than in a city, there are many men and women in the cities who give evidence that it is. Of course there are a few here who have missed altogether the distinction of being born in the State of New York. If no one will call the matter up against them, neither will any one deny that New York is a very good state for a New York University president to be born in. Chancellor Brown was not only born in a good state, but at a good time. He was born just at the time to get the name of a gallant young colonel of a New York State and New York City regiment, who was the first of a long line of hallowed sacrifices to give his precious life in the war to save the Union. Chancellor Brown in some way missed being educated in the New York schools, but he has been pretty well recompensed for it by life in a vigorous pioneer environment and by training in one of the very best State Normal Schools in the country, at Bloomington, Illinois, and at the State University of Michigan, a university which was the great leader of the state university movement in America, the most marvelous development of democratic institutions of real university grade that has appeared in the long history of world education. Spending a year in Germany, he

MORNING PROCESSION—DELEGATES ENTERING THE LIBRARY

Left to right: Walter Rautenstrauch, Esq., representing University of Missouri; Dr. F. W. True, Smithsonian Institution; President Eaton, Beloit College; Pro-Dean Sorapure, Fordham University; President Few, Trinity College (N. C.); President Woolley and Professor Kohl, Mount Holyoke College; President Hutchins, University of Michigan; President McClelland, Knox College; Dean Patterson, University of Louisville; President Davis, Alfred University; Professor Gillett, Union Theological Seminary; F. H. Kohlman, Esq., Tulane University; Robert Underwood Johnson, Earlham College; Professor Paton and Professor Mitchell, Hartford Theological Seminary; C. A. Williams, Esq., Oberlin College.

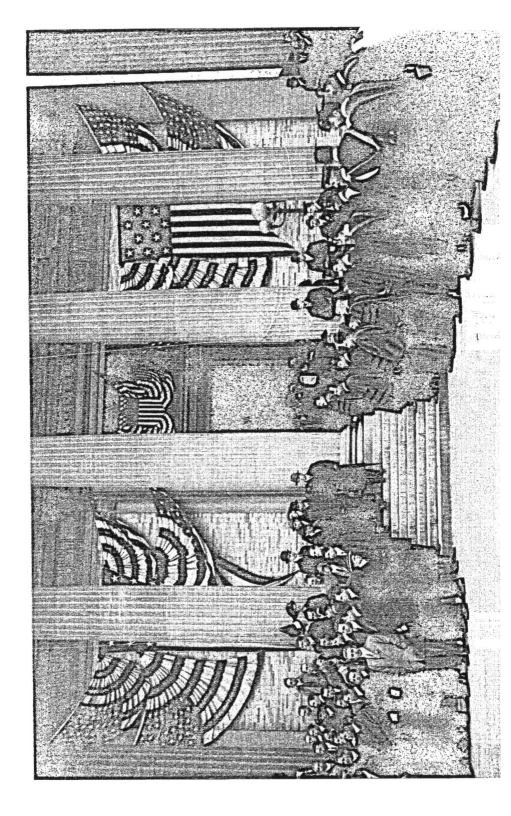

began teaching at the University of Michigan, and soon earned a professorship, which was continued at the University of California. This led him to know how states and universities may work together for the profit of each, a little better than all of us in New York realize. That knowledge produced the best history of the American middle-schools that has been written. Those are the schools of American creation which are at once the expression of our democracy and the connecting link in American education and which go further than any middle schools in other national systems of education to give all children their even chance. That book and the work that was behind it raised him to a place in the teachers' guild which is honored by all of the pedagogues and many of the people of the United States. In turn that lifted him to the office of United States Commissioner of Education, and it may be suspected that the call to your Chancellorship came in happy juxtaposition with his discovery of the tribulations, and perhaps the emptyhandedness, of an excellent teacher and a virile pedagogical author in pleading for needed appropriations at the hands of congressional committees. However that may be, it was high time to come home. It is splendid to go out West and gather up the thinking and the doings of pioneer people, and work with universities that express their highest aspirations, but it is well for the young men who do that to come home when they reach the place Dr. Brown has gained, and most certainly so if there are great universities in the home state that ask them to come and lead them. To be sure, not many of us have been accustomed to associate Chancellor Brown with a university presidency. He has seemed to fill the concept of a professor to the full, but we have never recognized the readiness to give pain or the strength to endure it which President Seth Low, when at the head of Columbia, used to say were the necessary attributes of a university president. We have never thought of the qualities in him which can deal with faculties as well as with students, and can speak to the public in such decisive and authoritative ways as we are accustomed to see setting so lightly on the shoulders of the successful university presidents. But we have no apprehensions. A good jurist may never be a great lawyer, but a great lawyer can cultivate the temperament and the habits of a first-rate jurist. Not all of the university presidents have the attributes of great teachers, but a real university will sustain a great teacher in the Chancellor's or the President's office; and it will be surprising if this one does not develop the ordinary attributes of his peers.

The state that chartered this University congratulates her upon calling such a son of the state back to his just inheritance and to her ennobling service. All in all, the day is a radiant one in the history of this University, and the State of New York expresses to New York University and to its new Chancellor the felicitations and the good wishes of the millions of people and of that mighty complexity of moral, intellectual, industrial, and commercial activities which enter into the Constitution and are concerned about the healthy life and the genuine progress of the Empire State."

RESPONSE FOR THE CITY OF NEW YORK

HIS HONOR WILLIAM J. GAYNOR, MAYOR

"Mr. Chancellor, Ladies and Gentlemen: I am very glad to be able to come here and participate in this occasion, but I can say only a word. I have listened with great interest to Dr. Draper's remarks, and after hearing him I am quite satisfied that in place of a board of education of forty-six in the City of New York, we could do with the number seven, which the last two charter commissions recommended, and possibly with even one, like the State of New York. After hearing him I am much in doubt whether the next charter commission may not recommend one, the same as the state has, and we will have another debate over the subject, with Dr. Draper no doubt on the other side of the question. New York, notwithstanding the many evil things said of her by those who want to say something bad of her, principally because they are bad themselves, has many things to be proud of, but she has nothing to be more proud of than her facilities for education. We have done our full duty as a people in that respect. Our universities, our colleges, our magnificent system of common schools, not excelled in the world, our libraries, our museums, our galleries of art, all combined, have an educational influence upon the people of this city that cannot in the long run or in the short run fail to be felt in the government of this city as well as in the social affairs of this city. I repeat that we have done our full duty in this respect as a people. I say duty, because the first duty of the citizens of a free government is to provide educational establishments. And I need not say to so intellectual an audience as this that free government, the formation of free government, the continuance of free government, depend entirely on the general diffusion of education among the people, from the university graduate down to the one who goes to the common grammar school. That is so of every free government, but it is far more so of the free government which depends on manhood suffrage, on universal suffrage, as we ordinarily express it. Because unless we can get a fairly well educated man—and that means a liberal man—not a little narrow-minded fellow that would vote a ticket because his grandfather voted it the same way—we cannot get a good result from universal suffrage. That may not be so of every vote, but it must be so of votes enough to control. In order to control sometimes votes may have to pass with great facility from one party to another year after year, and it is our aim to educate people who will do that and not merely begin to whine and say, 'Oh, my grandfather voted the Republican or Democratic ticket, and my father voted it, and I will vote it forever, and nothing else.' If our education comes down to that we are a poor lot indeed, aren't we? The career of the educated man has grown wider and wider, until now he enters into all phases of life. His horizon was once very narrow indeed. Shakespeare in 'Hamlet' expresses it, of the period in which that great play is cast. When speaking of the young men of that time, he said, stating where they had gone—'Some to the war to try their fortunes there, some to discover islands far away, some to the studious universities.' And that was all. That was the career of a young man at that time. There was nothing else open to him. Indeed, at one time there was nothing but the Church, because the preachers were doing everything, even curing us of our diseases, or trying to, and killing us in the bargain. But in the growth of God's time that is no longer so. By the force of education the center of thought has passed from the few to the many. Everything is now open to the educated young man. What Shakespeare said looks awful small to us now. Afterwards they went into what were called the learned professions. But now the phrase the learned professions is too narrow. It is too restricted and is misapplied, because we now have many learned professions. The mayor of this city appoints twenty-six heads of departments and bureaus for the government of the city. I suppose the President of the University of Chicago and some of our friends from the West who read certain newspapers, which God in His inscrutable reasons allows to be published here, think that those twenty-six people, including the mayor, are a lot of thugs. I do not know how they can think otherwise when they see the way they are spoken of and the way they are pictured throughout the country. But I beg to say on this occasion that nearly all of those twenty-six men are graduates of universities and colleges of high standing. I cannot enumerate them all; there are so many of them I cannot remember them myself, until I get them in a room and look at them. But there are Tomkins, and Thompson, and Waldo, and Murphy, and Watson—and so it goes—from Princeton, Harvard, Yale and other colleges and universities, and many of them from our own right here in the City of New York; I believe two-thirds or over. Everything is open to you, and I am bound to say you are taking everything. I do not say literally that you take it all, because there are some people in this world who, just like many of you, would get along even though you did not have the advantage of a university or a college education. I am reminded of that stilted observation of Gibbon, that 'the power of instruction is seldom of much efficacy except in those happy dispositions who would manage to get along without it.' I do not want to profess my literal belief in that. Those with the advantage of a college education have a great advantage over those who have it not, because those who have it not, but come within the literal term of Gibbon's statement, have to toil terribly to get it. They do get it, and maybe it is worth more when they do get it, but they have to work for it and work hard. It is often said in the legal profession that no lawyer ever comes to fame with á straight back or without a pale face. That is literally true of the young men who do not get their education in the universities, but get it by the light of their candle and by the terrible toil which I have mentioned to you. So much for the advantages of education. You enter the race with a great advantage in your favor. Make good use of it. Every one that goes out of a college or university has a sacred trust reposed in him, and those who come out not knowing that come out not knowing one of the most essential things that he should know in coming out. He owes a duty to society as well as to himself. He is not a man simply to come into any community to aggrandize himself and to satisfy his own greed. No, he owes the duty to society to watch public affairs, to participate in public affairs, to lift the community up, to do his part, in a word, as a good citizen to make the community in which he lives a good community and a well-governed community. If he fails in that he fails in the essential thing for which he was given an education. But you do not fail in it. Those educated in the schools of this country, the common schools, are prepared up to a certain point to be good citizens, and after them come others with a better education, until finally we reach the top—the university graduate. And those who know most and have the most virtue—to use a homely phrase which was much in use when I was a boy—slop over, as it were, and what they know and what they are is thus communicated to all society, and helps society and lifts it up, although they sometimes are unconscious of it. In the last analysis, they say, public sentiment is made by only a few people. I used to say by one person to each block in a city, and a man told me one day never to say that again to a popular audience, for they would all vote against me if I ever came up for office. I said, 'No, each man in the audience thinks he is that one in the block. So they will all take it as a compliment.' But, however that may be, public sentiment is made up of a few people. When a masterpiece is produced by the painter artist, who knows that it is a masterpiece? The great art critic of the last century is called in and he looks at it and he sees it is a masterpiece. Ruskin sees it and knows it and he brings in another, and finally twelve, maybe, see in it the masterpiece, because they are capable of judging it. And the opinion of these twelve slops over and finally becomes the universal opinion of all mankind. And so it is, and so it always has been with the learned man, and on a larger scale a collection of learned men in a university.

Now, I can say no more or you will think I am growing loquacious. So I will say nothing more but express again my good-will to this University and the feeling of pleasure which I have in coming here as Mayor to assist in the installation of your new Chancellor."

RESPONSE FOR THE EDUCATIONAL FOUNDATIONS

ELIHU ROOT, LL.D., '67, TRUSTEE OF THE CARNEGIE INSTITUTION; CHAIRMAN OF THE BOARD OF TRUSTEES OF HAMILTON COLLEGE; SENIOR UNITED STATES SENATOR FROM THE STATE OF NEW YORK

"Mr. Chancellor, Your Honor, Excellency, Ladies and Gentlemen: It is interesting that the name of Elmer Ellsworth should come to be the head of the institution which

half a century ago was made famous by Theodore Win-
throp in Cecil Dreame.

Notwithstanding the manly and vigorous voice that we
have heard this morning from the far distant past, there
are not many left under the sun who remember Chrysalis
College, in the fine gray old collegiate Gothic building on
Washington Square. As I look back to it as it was in the
early sixties and recollect the conditions which existed then,
the conditions of the University of the City of New York,
of the boys' schools, one called Columbia and one the Free
Academy of the City, and look across the long distance of
time and see what there is now, I am deeply impressed by
the fact that there has been a firm, steady, uniform, progressive development of the educational institutions of our country. There has been much free will for Presbyterianism to
lay hold of, but there has been more foreordination imposed
by the genius of free government, the natural and necessary
development of a free, self-governing people. The multitude
of impulses to promote religion, to minister to personal
vanity, to advance the fortunes of individuals, to add honor
to localities, to promote the development of particular
branches of science; all the great variety of impulses which
have led individuals to establish educational foundations,
have been working out results, quite independent of the
purposes, and forecasts of the individual founders. This
myriad of impulses, coming from individual will, has been
molded by the genius of a self-governing people into a
system out of which gradually are emerging systematic results. It has seemed as if our educational institutions have
had little or no policy. Indeed, they have had but little consciousness of an intentional policy. They have been following the course of their destiny, driven on by forces not understood by any man at their head, or even all of them put
together. Gradually we see emerging a differentiation of
our educational institutions. The old-fashioned college, the
institution, however, it may be improved and developed from
the germ of the old-fashioned college into the place of training for the whole man to make him ready for whatever
comes in life, is a separate class from the vocational institution, broadening and taking in its thousands of students,
filling their many separate desires to fit themselves for separate and special vocations in life. Now come the foundations designed for the enlargement of knowledge without
immediate and direct relation to the instruction of youth,
designed to relieve the men engaged in instruction from the

increasing duties of research, represented by the Carnegie Institution of Washington, which is one of the institutions I have the honor to represent here, so that research may be prosecuted, knowledge broadened, and excursions into the field of human possibilities undertaken far beyond the possibility of the institution whose first duty is to teach. As the multitude of the founders has increased, the spirit of the foundation has spread, and while Dr. Brown comes here from the western universities, he comes not from an alien system. The spirit of John Harvard and Elihu Yale and Eleazer Wheelock and Samuel Kirkland and all of that old and honorable list of men, who, centuries ago, devoted their substance and their prayers to the foundation of liberal centers of learning in our country, has spread through the multitude of donors, through the army of instructors, until it has permeated the great body of the people and through all the great West that spirit is interpreted by the people at the polls, who have established the great State institutions and are now sending back their sons and men of their training to broaden and invigorate the expression of that same spirit in the. older institutions. The western State Universities of Wisconsin, Michigan, Illinois, California and all the rest are the same thing that the individual founded long ago in the East expressed through the multitude who constitute government.

I cannot stop without saying one word of a contribution made to this University by the other educational institution which I represent here to-day, Hamilton College. Forty-five years ago, John Norton Pomeroy, of the class of 1847 of Hamilton, was at the head of the University Law School, and he was one of the few men who gave the impulse that has made the university what it is to-day, a noble, able, devoted, self-sacrificing instructor. A conspicuous illustration of that highest of all functions of the teacher, in that he presented to the young men of his time, the spectacle of a life made happy without wealth, without office, without any power except the power of natural sympathy, and with no reward but the joy of continually seeking and finding truth.

Chancellor Brown, I am sure that I can say for all the educational foundations of our state and our country, that you will find in them, in their officers, their friends, and their alumni, that sympathy and support without which no human power avails. In the republic of letters it is especially true that no man gains by the downfall of another. It is all up and none down, because schools of learning are participators in the wealth of all learning. There are no Tripolis in the education of the United States. I extend to you continual syr pathy, comradeship and God-speed."

RESPONSES FOR AMERICAN UNIVERSITIES

HARRY PRATT JUDSON, LL.D., PRESIDENT OF THE UNIVERSITY
OF CHICAGO

"It is with especial pleasure that I congratulate the new Chancellor on his induction into the administrative headship of an institution of learning situated in a great urban community. The obligations of a university under these conditions are of peculiar importance at this stage in the development of our country.

We must bear in mind the two-fold function of any university—the discovery and the dissemination of truth. The emphasis to be placed upon these respective parts of university duty and the content which may be given to each of these parts may well differ according to the location of the institution. In a great city with its crowded population, the limits of the university duties are to be conceived as co-terminous with the limits of the city itself. In other words, the university should not be content with the discovery only of scientific truth, which may have most direct bearing upon the city life, but should be especially industrious in the investigation and dissemination of such forms of truth as are directly related to the city. In this sense, in the first place, the university should be a repository of all such knowledge as may be needed by any branch of the city government—economic, political, scientific, educational. The university gathers within its walls a great body of experts in all these fields. The knowledge amassed in the university library and museums, and especially as energized by these groups of experts, should always be at the service of any branch of the city government. This of course does not imply that the university takes part in such political activities of the locality as might divide different portions of the electorate. It does mean, however, that all questions that have to do with fact should be susceptible of immediate and comprehensive answer within the university walls.

Of course, this same thing should be true also as related to groups of individuals. Organizations aiming at any humanitarian or economic purpose should be able to find within the university the solution of their various problems.

In short, the university should be a storehouse of knowledge for the use of the city in all its complex activities, and should have that knowledge in such shape as to make it immediately available at any time.

Further, an urban university has the very great advantage that it may use the city as a great laboratory for all its departments. This is true not merely of the manufacturing and commercial industries which every city supports. The economic and sociological departments of a university have a very great advantage in the means of study afforded by an urban population.

Thus an urban university has very peculiar advantages and very peculiar obligations. There is need, I am sure, in every large city of all the resources which can be afforded by all the universities which are, or are likely to be, established within urban limits; and therefore the New York University may share in one of the great works of the world."

EDMUND JANES JAMES, PH.D., LL.D., PRESIDENT OF THE UNIVERSITY OF ILLINOIS

President James responded on behalf of the State Universities. Unfortunately, owing to an oversight, a copy of his address was not secured for insertion here.

MARY EMMA WOOLLEY, L.H.D., LL.D., PRESIDENT OF MOUNT HOLYOKE COLLEGE

"Mr. Chancellor, a ceremony such as this to-day is in the nature of a coronation, to which we come as ambassadors. The Colleges for Women appreciate the honor of bringing a greeting and rejoice in the opportunity to wish for you a realization of all the high hopes for the future of this University, inspired by what it has already accomplished, by the promise of even greater achievement in the coming years, and by confidence in you as a leader.

Every thoughtful observer of English life and conditions last summer must have been impressed by the dramatic contrast between the pageantry of the coronation and the stern realities of ruling, which followed with such startling swiftness. Academic monarchs, Mr. Chancellor, have much the same experience. To-day, brilliant festivity, congratulation and acclaim—to-morrow the shouldering of heavy responsibility. This responsibility is heavier to-day than it was yesterday, will be heavier to-morrow than it is to-day. To train the youth of the country for 'employment in church and public state' was not as complicated a matter in 1701 as in 1911. And as the task becomes more difficult, in like proportion does the need become more imperative. The country has a right to make a high demand of our colleges and universities, in this age of perplexity and complexity, a demand that they shall train *men,* in the broadest definition of that word, not invariably scholars—it is doomed to disappointment if that is the expectation—but thinkers and workers, efficient, high-minded, sound in body and mind and soul, with a sense of responsibility for the common welfare. Nor is this high work for humanity exclusively the province of the colleges for men. All over the world there is a great sense of quickening in the social conscience, a great awakening in regard to the place and mission of women, in the body politic, in the body social, in the body religious. As representative of the women's colleges, I bring greetings from the institutions which have a responsibility not unlike that which is resting upon the undergraduate colleges for men, the responsibility of training *human beings,* not for any one special vocation, but for life, with physical and mental and spiritual powers so developed and disciplined that they are ready, wherever placed, to meet demands and master problems, to think straight and see clearly distinctions, intellectual and moral, and to live with the courage of their convictions. The particular vocation is incidental as compared with the larger issue. Efficiency and vision, there is no sphere of life to-day in which they are not needed, and the problem of the undergraduate college for women as well as for men is how best to meet this need.

Our greeting to you, then, Mr. Chancellor, is one not only of welcome and of good wishes for you, of congratulation for the University which has chosen you as its leader, but also of congratulation for ourselves, that your wide experience and high standards are to be devoted to the solution of the problems and the realization of the ideals of the American college."

JAMES HAMPTON KIRKLAND, PH.D., D.C.L., LL.D., CHANCELLOR
OF VANDERBILT UNIVERSITY

"I have been asked to say a few words as a representative of educational institutions founded by churches or private individuals.

The classification of institutions suggested by this request is, I trust, not very significant. There are differences in universities known by the distinctive titles of urban, state, church, or independent, but the points of agreement are larger than the differences. We may vary in origin, or in the sources from which we derive support, but the ideals, methods and agencies of our work are largely identical. The great educational forces of our whole country are one, and move as a unit in onward sweep and power. Perhaps the classification made is, after all, only a subterfuge for the selection of speakers, an expedient by which all voices may be heard, united in one grand chorus of acclaim on this joyous and auspicious occasion.

So I shall speak with as little regard to my constituency as a United States Senator after he has been elected to a long term. But if I tarry one moment by my supposed subject, I would pay a tribute to the religious agencies of this country for constant and abiding interest in educational enterprises. This influence was potent in the founding of Harvard, of William and Mary, and of all our earliest institutions. Some of these foundations have passed completely into the hands of independent boards; over some the churches still exercise a direct control; with others there is maintained a sympathetic union, a relation of historic interest and friendship, advantageous to both sides. But the one lesson taught by all this history is the vital connection between culture and character; between man the worker and man the thinker; between making a living and making a life; between mind and soul whose full accord is essential to that vaster strain whose swell shall encircle the planet. If this lesson is ever forgotten—which I consider most unlikely—the memory of our educational history should call us back to true ideals.

I bring to you, Mr. Chancellor, on this occasion the cordial greetings, the friendly congratulations, the sincere good wishes of a large number of colleges and universities. In these expressions of admiration and affection we are one. Your speaker comes from a long journey, the dust of the distant highway is on his garments. From the whole South, especially do I bring on this occasion personal and official greetings to you and to your institution. We remember gratefully your labors and ministries as leader of our national educational forces. With confidence we wait as you now lay your hand to new tasks. By the history of your own institution you are committed to an era of achievement

RESPONSES FOR FOREIGN UNIVERSITIES

JAMES BRYCE, O.M., D.C.L., LL.D., BRITISH AMBASSADOR; HON-
ORARY FELLOW OF ORIEL AND TRINITY COLLEGES, UNIVER-
SITY OF OXFORD

"Mr. Chancellor, Mr. Mayor, Ladies and Gentlemen: The privilege and the honor has been alloted to me of representing on this occasion the universities of other countries. I will not use the word 'foreign,' because that word would not apply to the universities which are more particularly represented here by my friend, the member of the Senate of the University of Toronto, as well as myself. We do not answer to the name of foreigners. Moreover, what has been said already by my friend, Mr. Root, is true. There is no distinction in respect of language, or tongue, or country, or form of government, between those institutions which are all devoted to the same high purpose. It is a particular pleasure to me to be the bearer to you, Mr. Chancellor, of congratulations and good wishes in the fulfillment of the duties that you are to discharge here, because it has been my privilege to know you in Washington, and to know what experience and what breadth of view in all educational questions you will bring to the work that awaits you here. It is a further pleasure, having seen for the first time the site in which this University is located, to be able to congratulate you all, Chancellor, and faculty, and students upon the splendid position which your buildings hold, looking out over this great populous region and on to the distant hills, where nature presents to you that amplitude of view that a university ought to bring to all human problems.

To be asked to speak for the universities of the European Continent as well as of England and Ireland, for I leave Scotland and Canada to my two friends who represent them, the Lord Rector of Aberdeen, and the member of the Senate of the University of Toronto—to be asked to speak on behalf of the universities of Europe, would be indeed a grave responsibility, if it were possible for me at this time to say anything worthy of such a long line of famous institutions, beginning from the school of medicine and the school of law in the University of Salerno and the University at Bologna in the eleventh century, and going on thence to the wonderful University of Paris, the greatest intellectual force in the Middle Ages, and all the other universities of Italy and Spain and those of Germany, from the University of Prague, down to those German universities of the eighteenth and nineteenth centuries, which have so largely helped to make the new German Empire. Of these I will not venture to speak, but will only add that I have been specially commissioned by the Vice-Chancellor of the University of Oxford to represent it here, as my own university, and to say that that older sister of yours—now eight hundred years old, but nevertheless, as hale and energetic as she ever was before—sends you her greetings and is glad to express her sympathy for your rising and expanding fortunes. She and all of the universities of Europe have the same common mission which you have, and there is nothing but friendly co-operation and sympathy between us all. As was said with equal force and truth by Mr. Root, there can be between institutions dedicated to learning and science no envious rivalry, nothing but a desire on the part of each that all the others shall flourish, because the good of each is the good of all. Our mission is the same now as it was in those early centuries, when the University of Oxford arose. In some ways the work that had to be done then was rather easier than that which stands before you and us now. The head of my college in Oxford, which was founded in the fourteenth century, and his colleagues in the headships of the other colleges of those days, were supposed to have done a great deal for their colleges, and built themselves a permanent name in their annals, if they had traveled to Italy and brought home a copy of a manuscript, probably of some work of St. Augustine or of Cicero. They were not expected, as you presidents and chancellors of American universities are expected now, to go about raising funds to build a new laboratory, or perhaps a new stadium. There was no trouble in those days about providing dormitories and lecture rooms, because the teacher lectured wherever he could find a place, possibly at the side of the street, and the students slept wherever they could find a roof to cover them. There were no elaborate organizations in those days. Everything ran itself, and there were fewer worries, especially about funds, and the presidents and professors of those days were not obliged to spend the best part of many a working day in sitting upon Boards and Committees. Modern universities have lost as well as gained something by the completeness and minuteness of the organizations they have created. Nor in those days was it necessary to take much trouble to find pensions for teachers who were retiring or who ought to retire. That difficulty has now been splendidly met by the munificence of one of our friends on this platform, who never did anything better for universities or the world than when he made his great educational foundation. In those days the problem was simple, for there was nothing to do but tell the teacher if he was getting a little past his work, that the time had come for him to retire into a monastery. There were plenty of monasteries at hand and as he was presumably unmarried what could suit him better? The main problem before every university is still the same now as it was then, to collect knowledge and to advance knowledge and to stimulate youthful minds, but there was a great difference in the attitude of youthful minds toward knowledge in those days. Universities were then like a few lamps twinkling amid the encircling gloom of ignorance which overspread Europe. Nowadays knowledge is everywhere. Knowledge of a sort is so diffused that people have come to think it cheap. Knowledge is like a diffused light spreading from the sky down over the whole world, even if it is for most people somewhat dim and hazy. And there is so much knowledge of the hazy kind, and every one is so fully persuaded that he is in possession of what he wants of it and there are so many voices and pens making things doubtful by their divergences that many people seem to have almost lost their interest in truth in the difficulty of discovering it amidst the enormous variety of fluctuating and discrepant opinions. This has made the task of the university not only more difficult, but more important than it ever was before, because the universities are the places where knowledge needs to be tested; where knowledge ought to be made thorough, and above all, where knowledge must be studied in the right spirit. In the Middle Ages, when there was so little knowledge, and it was so hard to get, there was an eager passion for it, which brought men from the farthest corners of Europe to the place where any famous teacher could be listened to, and made them hang upon his words, and nerved them to bear all hardships and sacrifices in order that they might obtain the precious gift of knowledge from his lips. But now the passion and eagerness seems very largely to be devoted to getting that kind of knowledge which is most useful not for mind and soul but for practical success in life. And so we feel in Europe—perhaps you too may feel it here—we feel in Europe that one of the chief things that the university is called upon to do, is to insist that although it is its duty to give instruction which shall fit men for all the practical business of life, qualifying them to do their professional work in the best possible way, upon the basis of the most accurate knowledge, still that is not the highest duty of the university, nor the duty in discharging which they will do most to help forward the progress of the world. The gainful occupations will take care of themselves, but the universities are especially called upon to hold up the highest ideal of the pursuit of knowledge and truth for their own sake. They must make men feel not only that the physical sciences will best advance and develop when they are studied in the abstract and in theory as well as with regard to their practical application, but also that truth is to be sought simply because it is truth whether any material benefit will or will not follow. The spirit by which discoveries are made, and the spirit which makes teaching stimulating and ennobling springs out of a disinterested love of knowledge and truth for themselves. This is the characteristic function and duty of universities. They are called upon to resist the pressure which is often put upon them to confine themselves to a narrow practical view of knowledge and of the intellectual aptitudes which serve gainful ends. The American universities, I am happy to think, have shown themselves alive to their duty in this respect and are most of them doing all that can be done to maintain the ancient and splendid ideals which inspired the universities of Mediæval Europe. You here in this great city have got an immense field open to you. Your mission in this vast commercial city is the same as we have in the cloisters of Oxford. It is a glorious mission with which the welfare of our race in our respective countries is bound up, and we here from our antiquity of eight hundred years, express to you our sympathy and our hopes, and wish you all success and prosperity in your work, a success and prosperity commensurate with the greatness of the city in which your lot is cast."

ANDREW CARNEGIE, LL.D., LORD RECTOR OF THE UNIVERSITY
OF ABERDEEN

"Ladies and Gentlemen: The home authority, responsible for my gorgeous robes upon this occasion, evidently thought that I should best promote the—what shall I say—the happiness of the family, if I were seen and not heard. The last three or four days I have been bearing my blushing honors thick upon me. There came the message from Aberdeen: 'You are elected Lord Rector. of Aberdeen,

AFTERNOON PROCESSION—SPEAKERS ENTERING THE HALL OF FAME

Left to right: Chancellor Brown, Mayor Gaynor, Borough-President Miller, President Judson, President James, President Woolley, Chancellor Kirkland.

A HALT IN THE AFTERNOON PRO

Last five persons: Chancellor Kirkland, Ambassador Bryce, Dr. Carnegie, D

without a contest, no opposition.' Mr. Mayor, that is the kind of a candidate you should select for an election. When you want a candidate next time for a position that has great honor and little labor, one that can get a walkover, I suggest to you I might be worthy of your consideration.

It is not customary in presenting addresses in Europe to accompany them by words. The oration is supposed to be within the roll presented. Therefore, my guide suggested that we should have the very telegram apprising me of my authority to act here to-day as Lord Rector for the first time—Mr. Chancellor, you are quite right—I trust it is not for the last. Herein (indicating a letter receptacle) is contained the identical message flashed across the Atlantic, three thousand miles under sea, giving me the great honor of being present here in my official capacity and this address, sir, I beg to present to you, hoping that it may be placed among the archives of your University, to show to future generations, centuries hence, that there was a University of Aberdeen, and that there was a young man named Carnegie, who was Lord Rector, and that his wife had the good sense to preserve the message, and that it was handed over to be held among the archives of this University, when it has a thousand years more added to its age.

I venture to say this for Aberdeen, and I know I express the sentiments of every one connected with it, that they have watched the history of your university, not with less favor, since it was known to have a little smack of Presbyterianism in it, for which we Scotch folks are remarkable. We trust, sir, that this University of Aberdeen, which already boasts four hundred years' existence, will double and treble this for it is that institution which more than any other university, even in Scotland, I believe, deserves to be remembered, and celebrated for the fact that its students cultivate literature on a little oatmeal. It is a poor university, as far as means are concerned, but it has a record, and the struggles that young men subject themselves to there, to earn its degrees, are indeed a daily wonder.

Let me tell you about Scotch universities. You know I gave them a gift, and I said to them that they should help struggling students and advance the fees of those who were worthy, but if in future years any of these students were successful and wisht to repay the advance made, not as a debt, but as a proud honor, I think in doing so they will be showing the love of independence so dear to the

Scot. Let me tell you it is only five years since that trust began. Last year I got letters from about fifty students; they sent me copies at my request, and they had paid back over fifteen hundred pounds (seventy-five hundred dollars) of the fees advanced, and this next year, so I am told by the actuaries, they believe that twenty five hundred pounds (twelve thousand five hundred dollars) will be returned by these poor students; and when I read their letters, wasn't I proud of my Scotch blood!

Mr. Chancellor, I beg to assure you that your elder sister university has watched your career; that it hopes you will still be engaged in the common work of leading the human race upwards—for all the centuries to come."

HON. WILLIAM RENWICK RIDDELL, F.B.S., LL.B., L.H.D., JUS-
TICE OF THE KING'S BENCH; MEMBER OF THE SENATE
OF THE UNIVERSITY OF TORONTO

"Mr. Chancellor, Ladies and Gentlemen—I feel peculiarly complimented upon being asked to address you this afternoon. I have not the very great advantage (teste Dr. Draper) of being born on a New York farm; but I did the best I could. I was born on a farm on the shore of Lake Ontario, almost in sight of the State of New York; and after I came to years of manhood and was dignified by the grant of Her Majesty's patent as one of her Counsel learned in the law, I had the pleasure on more than one occasion of representing this great State of New York in Her Majesty's Courts in my native province, thereby assisting to distribute the wealth of this State. And yet, while I feel highly complimented, 'nevertheless, I have somewhat against thee,' I am not wholly satisfied. (That is, however, the normal condition of a Canadian.) I do not complain but am proud indeed that I have been associated with speakers such as we have heard this afternoon, and especially that I have been associated with two brother Scots, one of whom continues, like myself, to be a British subject—and the other was once a British subject. I am placed beside my friend, Mr. Bryce, who is distinguished as statesman, historian and scholar, and Dr. Carnegie, whom I am proud to call friend, because he is the friend of all who, like him, are followers of the Prince of Peace. But what I do complain of is very much what was indicated by Mr. Bryce—that it is as a representative of a *foreign* university that I am presented. Now, I am a Canadian to the last drop of my blood. I was born under the British flag, and I come from a Canadian university; but there is no Canadian, at least no English-speaking Canadian, who considers himself a foreigner in this city or in this State. It is true that we are living in a land over which floats another flag, whose colors, red, white, and blue as they are, are differently arranged from the same colors on yours; and therefore from the standpoint of international law, we are aliens. It is true that it is the great nation across the Atlantic with which we in Canada are bound, politically and by that bond stronger than a band of steel, the bond of affection and ardent loyalty; but in all else we are to a great extent a part of the continent to which we belong. We are intimately associated with the people of the other part of that continent, both socially, commercially and financially; and why should we not be?

It is not in a physiological sense alone that 'blood is thicker than water'; and we are descended from the same ancestry. We have hundreds of years of history in common. Our language is the same. We all claim as our very own, Shakespeare and Milton. Our laws are almost identical; our institutions are similar. We have the like aspiration for liberty and justice, truth and righteousness.

From the Atlantic to the Pacific, for thousands of miles, stretches the longest international boundary on the face of the earth, and on neither side is there a fort which is more than a glorified farmhouse, a fortification which would not remind us children of the farm like you, Mr. Chancellor, and myself of the root house which used to be found upon every farm. We are pursuing our destinies in peace, side by side, working out our destiny in our own way. Our inland waters, pure as the heavens their source, bear the commerce of two peoples of one great race, one people, great now, and the other aiming to be great and determined to be great; but these pure waters are not polluted by any armed navy, or by any armed ships, except such as are sometimes heard of on political platforms, but never seen in war. It is for that reason, among others, that I am proud to be here.

Let no man suppose, let no man be persuaded that that good will which has prevailed between the people on this side of the international boundary and those on mine has been but on the surface, that the little storms on one side or the other have done more than clear the air and make the calm more grateful and serene.

And let no man be persuaded that the recent events in

Canada have any significance as indicating any diminution in the kindly feelings of my people toward yours.

The history of the commercial relations, the trade relations between the people of the United States and the people of Canada, either alone, or the people of Canada taken with their mother country across the Atlantic, has been a comedy of errors, in some instance almost grotesque. From the beginning, what one people wanted, the other refused, and when that other came around to a different view, then the first had also changed; and they were again at cross purposes. This whipsawing—I think that is the academic term—this whipsawing was expected to be brought to an end by the Elgin Treaty of 1854; but that was denounced in 1866, largely to punish the mother country vicariously through her daughter upon this side of the Atlantic; an easy method of dealing with a strong power. Then Canada, over and over again, urged the United States to grant her a renewal of the agreement. Her envoys were sent again and again to Washington. For sixteen years upon her statute book was a standing offer of reciprocity. Do not fear—I am not going to talk politics. As often as the envoys came they were received, sometimes graciously, sometimes the reverse: but their efforts ever were wholly in vain. At last Canada decided she would ask no more. With infinite labor, with infinite pains and splendid courage, of which I am proud, Canada forged out for herself new avenues of trade and new means of revenue, proving herself no unworthy daughter of the nation across the sea, a sister not unworthy to stand side by side with the greater and older and richer brother to the south; and when at length she had achieved to a certain extent that kind of trade independence which she desired and to which no other country is more entitled—for no country ought to be more independent—then came that overlong-delayed proposal. The majority of Canadian voters decided they were satisfied with things as they were. Forty-eight per cent. of the million and more who cast their ballots at the recent election thought they would like to accept the offer which had been made and made in good faith; fifty-two per cent. thought otherwise. Had three per cent. changed their views the result would have been different. Now I do not adduce that as any evidence of what I have been saying, that there has been no change of feeling. It has no significance one way or the other.

But it takes two to make a bargain. Canada is mistress

in her own house; and the American people would be the very last people on earth to desire to force anybody into a bargain simply because the American people desired to make it.

No more was ill feeling manifested by that election, or by the result of that election, than there was ill feeling in the heart of Americans toward the Canadians during the sixteen years or more in which we were making a standing offer of reciprocity, and in the many years in which our envoys were seeking from you a renewal of the treaty.

Now, let me not be misunderstood. I admit that there is in some parts of our Dominion an occasional individual who calls himself and perhaps believes himself to be a hater of the United States; but then I am informed that there are still in some remote parts of this great union some who believe they are haters of England. If there are some on our side of the international boundary—and they not always 'lewd fellows of the baser sort'—who like to take a shot at the American Eagle, the lion's tail is not wholly safe in some parts of your country.

We are intimately associated, sir, in educational matters as in all else. Our common or public school system in Ontario was based upon the common school system of Massachusetts. Our universities have taken much the same course of evolution as your universities upon this side of the line. True, in the University of Toronto, from which I have come, there are three separate arts colleges, each having its own faculty and its own senate, but the reason for that is historical; and the other Canadian universities in general have not that peculiarity. If I were to be asked, I would say that the University of Toronto in all else is more like a large American than a large English university. We have separate departments, faculties, post-graduate courses, college of medicine, and so on, and so on. We are pursuing the same end through much the same methods and by much the same means—or want of means, because our university, like every other university that is worthy the name, is poor and cannot get enough money. We have not yet in Toronto a Doctor Carnegie, although we are hoping to have one before the century is out. And our universities send their graduates to this side to fill the chairs in American universities, and we draw from American universities to fill our chairs; and there is nothing which you can do, there is nothing which can affect the university or university education or teaching in this great Union which

will not have its effect upon the University of Toronto. I
do not mean simply indirectly and by the influence which
the university would have upon the people of the United
States, through them upon the people of Canada, through
them ultimately upon the University of Toronto; but I
mean more directly, for in view of the solidarity of learning in the kingdom of letters, nothing can be done by one
sister, one subject, which will not affect, beneficially or the
reverse, the other.

And it is for that reason, Mr. Chancellor (but not alone
for that reason) that we are glad that you have accepted
the dignified and honorable position to which you have been
designated. We are glad that New York University will
not be checked in that high career which it has begun and
in which it has for so many years been running. We hope
and expect and believe that her future will be brighter even
than her past. My friends, it was no shoot from a wild
olive which was to-day grafted into this university. (I use
the word 'graft' in the horticultural and not the political
sense.) It was no shoot from a wild olive, as my friend,
the Chancellor, said, but it was a scion which came from
the very olive tree of Pallas Athene, beloved of Athens. No
such disaster has happened as when the Persian invasion
overwhelmed the City of the Violet Crown and burnt the
sacred olive of the Goddess of Learning; it was, indeed,
feared that the like had happened when Chancellor Mac-
Cracken resigned his position; but we hope and expect that
as that tree sent forth a shoot immediately after the retreat
of the Barbarian, which spread and spread and spread and
became a great tree, so you, sir, will be the new tree, the
new root from which a new glory will arise in this university.

We upon the other side of the boundary look upon
you in the United States, and in the universities of the
United States and in this university, not simply as neighbors
and friends, although that we believe you to be, not as
distant kinsmen or cousins, but as brethren; and we grieve
with you over your failures and we rejoice with you over
your successes. We watch with a brother's interest the
experiments which you are making in education, as in everything else. We are proud of the position which you have
taken and are taking and are to take in the world of learning, and we look upon these acts and achievements of yours
as the acts and achievements of our very brethren—and if I
correctly understand the feeling of my university, I say it is

the prayer of my university, as it is my prayer, that in this university there will be no backward step, but ever a pressing onward and onward toward the perfect day.

I bring to you the greetings and best wishes of the University of Toronto, and the other universities of the Dominion of Canada. I hope the best for this university: and the highest hope can go no higher than this: May the Chancellor be worthy of his university, and the university be worthy of its Chancellor."

THE INAUGURAL DINNER

The Inaugural Dinner was held in the Grand Ballroom of the Hotel Astor, at half past seven o'clock, and was preceded by an informal reception to the Chancellor and guests. More than two hundred visiting delegates and guests and six hundred alumni were present. The delegates and guests were seated with representatives of the Faculties and Council, at small tables next the Speakers' table; the alumni were seated by schools and classes. The invocation was pronounced by the Rev. Nehemiah Boynton, D.D. The souvenirs of the dinner were particularly appropriate consisting of a violet-covered book containing half tones of the seven University Chancellors, and of sorbet boxes in the form of a clump of violets. Reinald Werrenrath, '05, was present with a double quartet of University singers and led in the singing of the college songs. An especially pleasing feature of the musical program was the singing of the respective college songs immediately following the addresses by the various college representatives.

ADDRESSES

DR. GEORGE ALEXANDER, President of the University Council, acted as toastmaster and introduced the speakers as follows:

"Members and friends of New York University, honored guests, ladies and gentlemen: If the festivities of the evening are ended, the solemnities may now begin.

You men who call New York University Alma Mater, can appreciate the embarrassment of an alien forced into undue prominence in the exercises of this memorable day, by the accident of office or the grace of longevity. The best that I can hope, is that you will regard my failure to graduate at New York University as a youthful indiscretion, which may be partially atoned for by post graduate service.

The duty devolving upon me is a very simple one. I have to propose now the first toast of the evening and ask that you arise and drink to the health of the President of the United States."

[Toast to the President of the United States.]

"I have now the pleasure of reading a letter from the President.

THE WHITE HOUSE, WASHINGTON, D. C.,
October 28, 1911.

MY DEAR MR. KINGSLEY:

I have your letter of October 26th, and regret that my engagements preclude my attendance at the inauguration of Dr. Brown as Chancellor of New York University on November 9th. The government lost a faithful and valuable public servant when Dr. Brown resigned as Commissioner of Education, and the New York University is to be congratulated upon securing the services of so able and distinguished an educator.

I send you my best wishes for the success of the installation ceremonies.

Sincerely yours,
WILLIAM H. TAFT.

I have also to read a message sent by the Bureau of Education at Washington, with which Chancellor Brown has so recently been connected.

The Commissioner of Education and the entire staff of the Bureau of Education send hearty greeting and congratulations to you and to the University upon this auspicious occasion, and best wishes for a most successful administration.

P. P. CLAXTON, Commissioner."

[Numerous other letters and telegrams were received but could not be read because of lack of time.]

"And now it is my privilege to present to you the man who is the occasion of all of this disturbance to-day. He described himself this morning as a wild olive. He will be tame enough before we get through with him. Allow me to present to you Chancellor Elmer Ellsworth Brown."

N PROCESSION LEAVING THE HALL OF FAME AND MARCHING TO THE LIBRARY
hancellor Kirkland, President Woolley, Dr. Carnegie, Ambassador Bryce, Judge Riddell, Dean Stoddard.

PROCESSION ENTERING THE LIBRARY FOR THE AFTERNOON EXERCISES

ELMER ELLSWORTH BROWN, PH.D., LL.D., CHANCELLOR OF
NEW YORK UNIVERSITY

"Mr. Toastmaster and all the rest of you: My particular function to-night is to abstain from making a speech. This affair has been arranged by the alumni of the University, and it is perfectly well understood that what the alumni wish to-night, after all of the indulgences of the day, is to hear from the men not connected with New York University, who represent the friendly relations that we are fostering with other institutions; and so the New York University man is going to try to get through in a very short time.

Let me say to the Alumni that I congratulate you upon the success of this affair this evening. It is no secret, I think, by this time, that it is a very enjoyable, and a very bright, and a very successful affair. The word has been passed around freely here at this table, so I think I am giving nothing away. I congratulate you, and so far as I have a right to claim any part of it, I want to thank you very heartily.

There is one announcement of policy that I should like to make on behalf of the Council of the University, of which I chance to be a member. We are not announcing many policies in advance, but the time seems to have come to announce one, and it is this:

It has been decided not to conduct the affairs of the University permanently upon the lines followed this week. There is no mistaking the fact that we are having a fairly good time of it, but we don't expect to be able to run the University very long in just this way. Next week maybe, we shall get away from our festivities and get down to the ordinary crackers and cheese of every day work, and we shall be happy to have done so; but we shall be all the happier in getting down to the plain things of every day because we shall have such pleasant memories of these days of this week, and particularly of this day. And now, Mr. Toastmaster, I think the other speakers ought to have their chance."

THE TOASTMASTER: "As the spokesman for the University for the time being, may I ask you men of the University in the manner most approved among you, to endorse my words as I express our thanks to the distinguished guests representing various educational institutions, who have honored us by their presence here to-night.

(Cheers.) One of them remarked to me a few moments ago that he had never in his life sat in the presence of so many brains.

The most venerable of our American universities was nurtured in what I once heard Wendell Phillips call 'the thin air of provincial Boston.' Harvard is represented here to-night, not by her president, but by a member of her faculty, who is among us taking notes; in other words investigating the educational system of New York. I propose the health of Fair Harvard, and introduce Professor Hanus, her representative."

PAUL H. HANUS, B.S., LL.D., PROFESSOR OF EDUCATION,
HARVARD UNIVERSITY

"Ladies and Gentlemen: I have the honor to bring greetings and congratulations from Harvard University to Chancellor Brown, and to New York University upon this auspicious occasion. I regret extremely that it was impossible for President Lowell himself to bring you these congratulations and greetings, because I know how much pleasure it would have given him. I regret it also because I am here among a good many presidents of colleges, and I am nothing but a professor; and in the second place, I am one of those unfortunate persons, who make their best after dinner speeches on the way home, after the occasion is over; and finally, I am only a professor of education— it used to be called 'pedagogy'—a subject which has not yet attained universal academic respectability.

However, I am also delighted that I happen to be the representative of Harvard University on this occasion, just because I am a professor of education. Your distinguished Chancellor, as it happens, began his university career as a professor of education—as a professor of x; for education as a university study was at that time an unknown and undetermined quantity. Education was a newcomer among university studies, and the representatives of the new study, as well as that study itself, were looked upon with some suspicion, and sometimes almost with aversion. It was one of Doctor Brown's achievements that he helped to allay this suspicion in the two institutions with which he was connected, the University of Michigan and the University of California. His distinguished services in the field which he then occupied helped to make the study of education respectable. I speak advisedly, ladies and gentlemen. Those of you who look upon the activities of the university in the field of education to-day will scarcely realize what a struggle had to be undergone in order to wring from the university faculties of this country an appropriate and adequate recognition of the importance, the magnitude and difficulty, and the complexity of the problems with which the university professor of education has to deal; and an acknowledgment of the seriousness of that study as a university study.

It is odd, but true, that one of the most distinguished universities of this country established its courses in education, decided what should be taught in them, and then invited the professor to take the chair; and none of the courses could be counted toward a degree. If any students elected the courses in education no harm should come of their misguided interest! Among the things that the professor had to do when he assumed the direction of affairs was gradually to kill most of the courses that had already been decided upon, and to substitute in their stead other courses that seemed to be more reasonable and more likely to be commensurate with his responsibilities.

But I am talking about what is now ancient history. That was twenty years ago. Since that time an appreciation of the duty of the university to study education—that activity on which human progress so largely depends, has been achieved; and there are very few self-respecting universities in the country to-day that are not seriously studying the subject, or that are not preparing to study it.

I am not here, however, to discuss at length the struggle which this new study of education had to find its place among the established university studies. I want in the few minutes at my disposal rather to draw your attention to the new forms which this study of education has assumed.

I suppose there is no subject in the world which has so many specialists as education. I have observed that business men, and lawyers, and physicians, when elected to a board of education or to a school committee, as we say in Massachusetts, immediately become specialists in education. It is not likely that if these men were put on a board for the construction of a railway, or a board for the development of a hospital, or a board for the development of some business enterprise, with the details of which they were unfamiliar—it isn't likely that they would at once develop the specialist's knowledge and express the specialist's judgment in those fields, as they often do in the field of education. That is a strange fact; but the reason for it is not far to seek.

It is fortunately everybody's lot in this country to be educated, to some extent at least. Sometimes a man is subjected to it under compulsion, to be sure; but it is nevertheless his lot. He consequently grows up with the idea that he knows something about education, just as every one grows up in this English-speaking land with the idea that he knows something about the English language. Now, we learned long ago to distrust that general knowledge, and to insist that if a man is to know the English language, he must study the English language, he must practise the English language, he must understand how the English language is to be used and have abundant opportunity to use it. Well, as I said, in the field of education everybody is ready to express an opinion; and unfortunately, until very recently the professors of education and students of education, like all the rest, could rely only on opinion with respect to educational affairs. And to the present day that is largely true. We are, however, trying to learn to put behind opinion established truths. To-day, on most matters of education your opinion is as good as mine; mine is as good as yours, and neither of them is good for much when it comes to using our opinions as a guide for practice. The reason for that is the reason which I have indicated, namely that even as specialists, we are still in the realm of opinion, where the layman's opinion is as good as the professional man's, and the professional man's opinion is no better than that of the layman.

Now, I don't want to be misunderstood; I have exaggerated a bit, of course. It must certainly be true, almost always, that the man who devotes himself to the study of education will acquire opinions that have more value than the opinions of the man who has not studied education. Nevertheless, it still remains true that we are just beginning the development of a science of education. It is only a little while ago that we had no science of psychology; it is now a rapidly developing science. So it has been and is with the formative science of education. Perhaps what I have been saying will be more intelligible if I give one or two illustrations—very elementary they will seem to you; but they will serve my purpose all the better on that account.

If any half dozen people in this room were asked how much arithmetic a boy fourteen years of age knows what would those half dozen people say? If they were asked how well he ought to know it, what would those half dozen people say? If they were asked how much arithmetic he ought to study, there would probably be half a dozen different opinions, and if they were asked how well he ought to know it, there would probably be as many more. My point is this: That since we haven't found out how much arithmetic a boy of fourteen knows, we don't know how much time it takes him to learn it, and we don't know what methods it takes in order to get him to learn it. In other words, we have not experimented in education to establish facts on which we can rely, as the surgeon has experimented to establish the facts on which he can rely; as the engineer has established facts on which he can rely; and as the psychologist is coming to establish facts on which he can rely. My point then is, that in the field of education, one of our problems is the setting up of well-organized, carefully checked, appropriately appraised experiments to settle general opinion.

Let me give one other very homely illustration: If you were to ask your neighbors—any one of you—whether it was a good thing for a boy or girl to study English grammar, you would probably get a variety of opinions. If they were asked also how much grammar the boy or girl ought to know, you would probably get another set of opinions; and your opinion, like his opinion, would be good for little or nothing in determining the question at issue.

Now, how shall we find out? Suppose we have ten schools over here, in which the principals are interested in teaching grammar as well as it can be taught. Over here are ten schools in which the principals are indifferent with respect to the amount of grammar a pupil ought to learn. Suppose those two groups of principals were encouraged to teach the English language, with or without much English grammar, as they prefer, for a series of years; and suppose that during the time that this experiment is in progress —say five years—it is carefully watched; and at the end the results in the use of the English language and the facility with which the pupils acquire a foreign language are judicially appraised. Don't you think we would know a great deal more about what English grammar is good for than we know now?

These illustrations are very homely and very element-ary, as I have said, but unfortunately they indicate new procedures in the field of education, to establish or refute the most elementary, the most widely accepted or con-troverted opinion. So, we might go on with a variety of other illustrations. We would like to know, for example, whether a board of education consisting of seven members is better than a board of education consisting of forty-six members. We have gathered in this city, as you know, a large amount of opinion on that subject, and we have really convinced nobody. The only way to find out whether a board of seven is better than a board of forty-six, is to have the working of a board of forty-six carefully inquired into, and a board of seven carefully inquired into; and to do that not in one place, but in a good many. I am using forty-six, because that happens to be in my mind, but take twenty-six, or twenty, or any number you please. My point is that the thing to do is to find out by careful investigation, by inquiry, how a board consisting of twenty-six members works. Find out by careful inquiry how a board consisting of seven works; and do that for a number of places and over a series of years, and set your facts forth in such a way, that he who runs may read.

I don't want to take more than my proper time, Mr. Chairman: but before I sit down, I want to say three things: First, that one of the great obstacles to educational advance in this country, and in every country for that matter, is complacency—self-satisfaction; second, that the way to get rid of complacency, and to make progress, is to set going the habit of self-examination; and third, that in order to get out of complacency and to realize the progress we are after, is to set going well-conducted, well-organized, well-checked, and well-appraised experiments. In that way we shall tend to break up the autonomy which every great school system, and many a small school system acquires, and shall see clearly in education not merely an important routine, but the problems underlying that routine, and work progressively toward their solution. In closing, I wish once more to congratulate this University heartily on its acquisition of Chancellor Brown, and to congratulate Chancellor Brown on the opportunities which the Chancellorship affords him. And finally, I want to suggest to Chancellor Brown that one of the ways in which it seems to me the University can render most conspicuous service to this community and to this country, is so to manage his trustees and the friends of the University, that they will help him to undertake the self-examination, destroy the complacency, and set going the experiments in the field of education to which I have referred. Thus will the University contribute its share, and play an increasingly important rôle in the progressive development of that science of education which we all hope is near at hand."

THE TOASTMASTER: "We most heartily welcome to our

AFTERNOON PROCESSION—THE DELEGATES MARCHING THROUGH THE HALL OF FAME

Honorary Marshal Victor J. Dowling, LL.D., '90; Dr. Fletcher B. Dressler, representing U. S. Bureau of Education; Assistant Commissioner Augustus S. Downing, representing New York State Education Department.

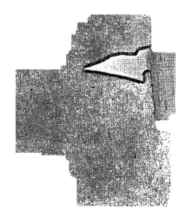

AFTERNO(
Faculty o

company to-night, Eli. I propose the health of Yale, Mother of Men, and her President, Arthur Twining Hadley."

ARTHUR TWINING HADLEY, PH.D., LL.D., PRESIDENT OF YALE UNIVERSITY

"Mr. Toastmaster and Chancellor Brown, Ladies and Gentlemen :—

When I first heard that it was suggested that New York University should take away from the National Government the head of the Bureau of Education, I hardly knew what to do more, to commiserate the Bureau of Education or to congratulate New York University.

In the blanks for information which are sent by various agencies to all of us for the recommendation of candidates for positions, the first question usually is: 'Have you seen the candidate actually at work?' I have seen the candidate actually at work, and I have seldom seen a man who works to so much purpose.

I had occasion not long ago to investigate the scientific work done in various bureaus at Washington. The Bureau of Education was not one of those investigated. On the contrary it was one that helped me in the investigation. But I was impressed with the fact that no other bureau was organized as efficiently as the Bureau of Education, under the gentleman whom we to-day salute as Chancellor. Working with small resources on large problems, he had so ordered the service as to do twice and three times and four times what any of his predecessors had done, and he had so encouraged those under him with his support, that they learned to do the work in the way that he did, and to get results from it. As he takes up the duties of his new position I congratulate New York University especially on the fact that he is a man who not only does but also looks for results.

In the experimenting that we are doing on education to-day, we all of us are tempted to lay too much stress on the process, and too little on the product. Mr. Brown and Mr. Hanus will know best how difficult it is to make our measures measures of efficiency, instead of measures of knowledge or measures of industry. A French essayist has said that virtue is more dangerous than vice, because its excesses are not subject to the restraint of conscience. In educational matters we perpetually have to see and feel the truth of this principle. The industry itself seems so meritorious that there is a tendency to overuse it and to waste it. The getting of knowledge seems so good a thing that there is a tendency to clutter up the mind with knowledge which has been slowly and laboriously acquired, but which, with the limitations that we all of us know human intelligence has, tends to keep other knowledge out. One of the leading educational authorities says, in discussing the requirements for admission to college, that education in geometry should begin in the kindergarten, and go on continuously; in other words, that it should take twelve years. This is eleven and a half years too much. What can we do with such slowly and laboriously acquired knowledge? Far better to take a half year to train the boy to fix his attention on a subject, to get work done, to be in a position to do things. In after life he will not have twelve years to master his law cases in; he will not have twelve years to decide on the diagnosis of his medical cases. We want to develop not merely knowledge and not merely industry, but mental efficiency. The danger by which we are beset, the danger by which men in the educational profession are more beset than anybody else, is to measure our work by the amount of knowledge gained, instead of measuring it by the amount of power gained.

Gentlemen, I congratulate you that the new head of New York University as an educator merits this superlative praise, that, from the beginning to the end, he knows the difference between a stuffed bird and a live one."

THE TOASTMASTER: "Among the universities represented here to-night, the third in the order of seniority is 'Old Nassau.' Are you all guessing who is going to be her president? Her representative is Professor William Francis Magie, whom it is my pleasure to introduce."

WILLIAM FRANCIS MAGIE, A.M., PH.D., PROFESSOR OF PHYSICS, PRINCETON UNIVERSITY

"Mr. Toastmaster, Mr. Chancellor, Ladies and Gentlemen:—

When your very energetic secretary, who is also my very pleasant table companion, asked me to speak a few words to you this evening, I at once set about trying to follow his advice as well as I could. I went to a very dear friend of mine who often gives me advice, and I asked him how I could succeed, what I ought to do in order to make this speech and say a few well-chosen words. He wouldn't give me any help at all. All he would tell me was a speech he once heard made by a distinguished man at Oxford. It was at a public dinner which had lasted till twelve o'clock. Finally Professor Mahaffy, the famous Irish wit of Dublin, was called upon to speak. He was noted for his eloquence. He arose and said: 'Gentlemen, at this time of night the finest eloquence is silence.' I thought that was a splendid lead for my speech. I thought perhaps being a professor I should come on after these distinguished college presidents who are on this list, and I thought perhaps it might be twelve o'clock before I was called upon, so that I could try the same method as Professor Mahaffy. I was pretty sure that if my old friend, the President of Columbia, only could get going before I came on, he would run on until twelve o'clock without much doubt. As that is not the case, and as I have to take the precedence, which comes from my being connected with the third oldest of the colleges that are here represented, I shall certainly have to do something more than that.

As I was sitting in the exercises this morning, several things occurred, several things were said, which raised thoughts in my mind, upon one or two of which I should like to say a word. In the first place, I was shocked by the remark made by your honored, your venerated Ex-Chancellor about the State in which Princeton happens to be, which also is the State in which I happen to have been born, and of which I have been a citizen ever since I was born, the State of New Jersey. He treated that State of New Jersey just exactly as if New York was a first-class European power, and New Jersey was on the other side of the Mediterranean. He annexed the most important part of New Jersey in population, simply in order to amplify the population of the City of New York. We New Jersey men always have felt that curious sensation of being thought of as in a foreign and inaccessible country. It always has seemed to me that to the New York men New Jersey is at an infinite distance; that the Hudson River is not only unnavigable, but a thousand miles deep; that the Palisades cannot be flown over with the best aeroplane and that the salt meadows, if you tried to get over them, are simply impassable. New Jersey is altogether out of your world. When I heard those gentlemen speak who were called upon as the representatives of foreign universities, I felt that I certainly should stand in precisely the same position. In fact, I thought I should represent to-night the only foreign university that would have the privilege of speaking at this table.

But, after all, as the speeches went on, it interested me very much to find in how many respects the history of Princeton and the aims of Princeton and the condition of Princeton resemble those of the New York University. We were started years and years ago by a little body of Presbyterian ministers, mostly Presbyterian ministers, not all, by laymen and others who were of other denominations, but we were started as a protest against the too rigid theology of New England. We were maintained, as the New York University has been maintained, for a long time largely by the support of that great ecclesiastical body, the Presbyterian Church, though we, just as the New York University, have had ever since our beginning the distinction, I think it is the almost unique distinction among the older institutions, of being from the beginning free from any restriction as to theological or denominational connection in our body of students, in the faculty, and in the Board of Trustees. We have always been, as you are, free from any such connection. We have grown, as you have grown, so as gradually to loosen the bonds which connected us with a particular denomination and to make our connection with the general world somewhat more free, somewhat more complete.

And then another thing: Princeton is distinctly a country university. It is one of the things we are very, I won't say proud of, because you can't be proud of the fact that you happen to be in one place rather than in another, but a thing we are very well satisfied with. There are a great many things that are pleasant and good about a country university. All of the professors don't have to be so careful to keep the creases in their trousers. The students don't have to be quite so careful about the way they dress and go about. I think it is a little easier for a poor man probably in a country university, and if we don't have plenty of poor men in our universities, we lose a great deal. Then I think it is a good thing, too, that the country university has its play and its work pretty closely connected. Here on your campus of New York University you have a football field that is a good deal nearer your work rooms than our football field is. Of course it is easier for me to get to the golf links. I don't believe the professors here have quite such an easy time as I do in that respect. But still in this new place, this place upon which you have at last, after so much striving, succeeded in placing your university, in this new place you do have this feeling of being in the country, being in a place where you have room to expand. I tell you the time has gone by when a German prince could set aside an old palace he was tired of, appoint a dozen distinguished men as professors and start a university. That time has gone by. It is especially on account of the diversity of studies, which need enormous plants, which need laboratories and buildings in which experiments can be carried on that our universities are demanding plenty of room. You cannot have those things, at least you can't have them where you can get at them without room. We can see this tendency to spread out even in the great universities that happen to be in cities. They are all trying to get out to the borders. Johns Hopkins is moving out to the suburbs of Baltimore. Yale, I think, has just put some of its most important recent buildings at a distance from the old university, and you have done exactly the same thing. You have got out to a place where you have a lot of room. I congratulate you and I congratulate the distinguished gentleman under whose guidance that result was attained, that you have succeeded in getting a place like that, where you can spread yourselves a little, where the self-consciousness of the university can have a chance to develop.

I was talking with a young man whom I know very well, a recent graduate of this institution, who knows Princeton too. He told me that the life here in the university on the Heights was very much the same sort of life as that we have, and I felt that I could in that way have a sympathy with you and with your life that it would be difficult for me to have in other cases. I wish to congratulate you upon having that opportunity to have this country life.

Mr. Chancellor, I wish to convey to you from the Faculty of Princeton University, from the Trustees and from all of us, our most hearty congratulations on your selection to this high office, and our sincere hope and expectation that your administration will be crowned with the most abundant success."

THE TOASTMASTER: "In his inaugural address this morning, Chancellor Brown expressed the hope that the universities and colleges in this city might confer for the advancement of education within its bounds. That conference is about to begin. The time has passed for competition between the universities and colleges of the City of New York, when their halls are crowded beyond the possibility of properly caring for the students who are flocking to their doors and are going to flock to their doors in ever-increasing numbers. I propose the health of Columbia. May her

shadow never be less, and I present to you as her representative, the Educator, Publicist, Diplomat, Messenger of
Peace, President Butler."

NICHOLAS MURRAY BUTLER, PH.D., LL.D., LITT.D., PRESIDENT OF COLUMBIA UNIVERSITY

"Mr. Chairman—I direct your attention to the subtle skill
with which my old friend Magie, having first distracted
your attention by an anecdote relating to the substitution of
silence for oratory, proceeded to leave me but one hour
and twenty minutes before midnight!

I became very much alarmed at one time this afternoon
at the solemnity of the functions on the Heights. The very
earnest exhortations and orations began to make me think
that instead of having come to a baptism, I had arrived at a
funeral; but those fears have been removed by the cheers
and the songs and the very appropriate note of levity which
has now been introduced into this occasion. Because, Mr.
Chancellor, I want to tell you that being a college president
is great fun. You must not believe all these serious things
they have been telling you. There is really nothing like it.

In the first place, a college president lives on a diet of
professors. He eats a professor of sociology for breakfast
preferably, and if your wife is discreet, you have a man
in literature for dinner. It is a really admirable
and nutritious diet. In the second place, I assure you
that in the course of a year you will meet or hear from
one-half of the wise men and all of the lunatics in the
community.

Then, in the next place, you will, if you are as well
equipped for the post as I believe you to be, speedily become
a liar. All college presidents are liars *ex officio*. I remember some years ago that when my dear friend, Dr. Canfield, became Chancellor of the University of Nebraska, he
was called a liar by a local newspaper or by some conten-
tious person within thirty days. He was walking with
President Eliot of Harvard one Sunday afternoon, while
we were all together attending an educational meeting, and
Mr. Eliot said to Dr. Canfield, 'Well, Canfield, I see that you
are a liar?' 'Yes,' said Canfield, 'I am;' and added, 'I suppose, Mr. Eliot, they have often called you a liar?' 'Oh!'
said Mr. Eliot, 'worse than that; they have proved it.'

A little while afterward 1 told that story to the late
Senator Hanna of Ohio. I wanted to indicate to him that

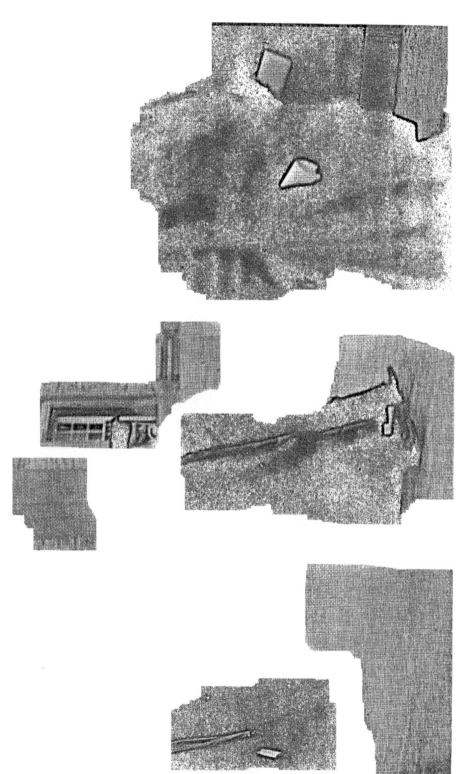

CHANCELLOR KIRKLAND, PRESIDENT WOOLLEY, DR. CARNEGIE AND AMBASSADOR BRYCE

politicians had no monopoly of this one of the fine arts. 'Oh,' he said, 'let me tell you a story that will illustrate just how that reputation of being a liar arises.' He said that when he went down to Washington with Major McKinley after his election to the Presidency, he met a friend of theirs from a small town in Ohio, who came up to him and said, 'Why, Mr. Hanna, congratulate me.' Mr. Hanna replied, 'On what?' 'Why,' answered the man, 'I am going to be Ambassador to Italy.' 'Ambassador to Italy, you!' 'Why, certainly,' he said, 'certainly.' 'Why,' asked Senator Hanna, 'what makes you think so?' 'Well,' was the reply, 'Major McKinley promised it.' 'Oh, I know,' said Mr. Hanna, 'but what did he *say?*' 'Why, we were talking about it, and he just promised it.' 'I know,' insisted Mr. Hanna again, 'but you can recollect the conversation; what did he *say?*' 'Why,' I said, 'Major, I have been a friend of yours, and I have supported you always, and I thought I would like to ask you if perhaps I could have an appointment?' 'Why, certainly,' said the Major, 'I think so; what would you like?' 'Well,' I said, 'I have been looking through the red book, and I sort of picked out the Ambassador to Italy; and then—then he promised it to me.' 'I know,' said Mr. Hanna, 'but what did he *say,* when he promised it to you?' 'Why,' he said, 'John, what an idea!' Forever after that man believed Major McKinley was a liar, for the ambassadorship never came his way.

You may have observed, you have not had time to read the newspapers to-day, that the gentlemen who collect the ashes and the garbage in this town have gone on a strike, because they do not want to work at night. I say to you now that you need not try that. The rules of our union are a minimum sixteen-hour day, and the only poet who ever understood what we have to do was Rudyard Kipling. He did not write it about college presidents, but that was, I think, merely a slip of the pen. You remember he wrote about a certain type of human being in whom he was interested, and said:

'His work begins at God-knows when; his work is never
　　through.
He doesn't belong to the regular line, and he isn't one of
　　the crew. . . .
You can leave him at night on a bald man's head to
　　paddle his own canoe;
He is a sort of a blooming cosmopolouse, soldier and
　　sailor, too.'

And you will find, my dear Chancellor, that Mr. Kipling hit it about right. You will be surprised at the questions you will be asked, and that you will answer; because omniscience is necessary, absolutely necessary, in the office of college president. If you flinch in the face of a question you are gone. You must know all about it—at least till you can get away.

Of course, there are persons who have quite a different idea of this office, but they are always persons of one of two kinds: either those who have held the office and do not hold it any more, or those who have wanted to hold it and have not held it. Both kinds have an angle of vision that interferes a little with looking the facts in the face. The real fact of the matter is that to be a college president is the greatest fun in the world. You associate with the best human beings that there are. You see them at their best. You try to do things that every intelligent man and woman in the universe believes are worth doing, and everybody who has got a soul or a brain bigger than the head of a pin wants to help you.

Despite the seductive picture of a golf course, which Magie drew just now—because you *can* get to a golf course from here—I am glad you have come to town. I have not so much opinion of these country places where they do not have pavements and water supply and various other things. I have a weakness for comfort.

Let me tell you a little about this town. It is a very queer place. Everybody in New York and outside of it abuses it, but they all like it pretty well. There is a sort of feeling that in order to prove that you are a loyal New Yorker or loyal American, you must say something disagreeable about New York. For instance, some disagreeable man says that the subway is noisy, that the elevated roads darken the streets, and that the streets themselves are torn up. Just look for yourself and see. Those statements are without any basis, in fact. Of course, they have to lay a pipe, I suppose, now and then, even in a city; but as a general rule, I mean, you will find here all the attractions and comforts of a simple Christian home.

Then, you will find people to talk to. I predict that you will make three hundred speeches in the next twelve months, and that after declining seven invitations out of eight. You will find companionship and society of all sorts and kinds; and after you have been enjoying it a little while, if you are turning through the pages of your Longfellow, you will come some day upon this, and you will do what I did—you will cut it out and paste it on a cardboard and put it on your desk, because it is splendid and it is true. Longfellow wrote these words: 'Where shall the scholar live, in solitude or in society? In the green fields, where he can hear the heart of nature beat, or in the dark gray city, where he can feel and hear the throbbing heart of man? I make answer for him, and I say, in the dark gray city.'

I am glad, my friend, that your lot is going to be cast in this city. Do not be worried about its extent, about the complexity of its population, about the excellence of its government, about any of the problems that are connected with it, for they are the temptation, the inducement, and the incentive, to doing things that are really worth while. There never was, there never has been in modern times such a theater, such a platform for educational activity and influence, as is afforded by this great metropolitan community at the beginning of the twentieth century. Pouring in through these gates come the great populations of Europe, settling here to learn our institutions, to become part and parcel of our body politic, to catch the spirit of our civilization and our laws, and to help those who came first to work out the great problem of democracy at the gates of the continent. Where can you work with a longer lever than here? Where can you help raise a heavier weight, and from what fulcrum can you exert a mightier force? I say to you, my friend, friend of many years, there is no room in American education for institutional competition. There cannot be, there dare not be; for with every institution in this land bound together as a unit, we would yet be feeble before the task that nature and human nature have set us. It is madness to suppose that every man, every force, every element of progress and uplift is not needed. We need it all, and by working together in close sympathy, with complete understanding, before our generation closes we can make this New York what it ought to be—not merely one of the world's great centers of population; not merely one of the world's great centers of commerce and trade and industry and finance and accumulated wealth; but one of the world's great beacon lights, where the things of the human spirit, the things that find expression in words, in deeds, in the achievements of art, and letters and science, in human institutions, are held up as the goal, not only for our dear America, but for all the world. God bless you, as you put your hand to your share in that stupendous task."

THE TOASTMASTER: "I invoke your sympathy with President John H. Finley in the fresh bereavement which deprives us of his presence here to-night, and leaves him fatherless. In silence may we drink to the health of President Finley and the College of the City of New York."

[Toast to President Finley and the College of the City of New York.]

THE TOASTMASTER: "One of the youngest of our universities, whose phenomenal growth has almost overshadowed the State of New York, is Cornell University. I propose a health to Cornell and to her President, Doctor Schurman."

JACOB GOULD SCHURMAN, A.M., SC.D., LL.D., PRESIDENT OF
CORNELL UNIVERSITY

"I desire, Mr. Chancellor, to present to you not only my own personal greetings, cordial as they are, and naturally as they grow out of our acquaintance and friendship, but also the greetings and good wishes of Cornell University, and the assurance of our desire to co-operate with you, and with our sister institutions in the State and out of it, for advancing the great work to which we are all dedicated.

In spite of the levity in which my friend Butler has indulged in his admirable speech, your office is a pretty difficult one. I believe Mr. Roosevelt said that the presidency was a bully place to preach from. Well, the presidency of a college or university offers, as Brother Butler has said, innumerable opportunities for speeches. But there is a lot of hard work in it, and there are difficulties inherent in the situation of American universities, difficulties peculiar to this country. I think the presidency of an American university is, with the exception of one or two public positions, the hardest office in the United States. And it is the hardest because the president has to deal with so many different problems and get on with so many different sets of men. The American university is composed of heterogeneous elements, bound together no doubt for a common purpose and engaged in a common work, but heterogeneous they remain. The members of the institution look at things necessarily from different and often opposing points of view. The point of view of a member of the board of trustees, Mr. Chairman, as you perhaps know, is very different and often radically opposed to the view of a professor. In nine cases out of ten the professor is right and the trustee is wrong;

but the trustee holds the whip hand, because he controls the finances, and the president has got to get on reasonably well with both the trustees and the professors. The professors look at everything as they should from the point of view of the ideal,—of scholarship, science, and culture. The board of trustees often look at everything from the point of view of dollars and cents, and many of them think no more of decapitating a professor than of dismissing a cash-boy. Yet, no university in this or any other country can be conducted on the principles for which such trustees would stand. Then the president has to deal with the alumni and the students, again different groups with different points of view. Here to-night are college and university professors and presidents galore. Haven't we all had experience of the fact that when some great and important change is made in the curriculum, many old students and alumni see in the beneficent change a sign of deterioration and decay? 'Things are not what they used to be when I was a student at the university!' Or, again, look at the matter from the point of view of the students. A court in taking evidence puts on the witness stand, not the offenders themselves, but others, and asks them questions. That violates the student's sense of propriety. It is dishonorable for him to tell anything about his fellow students. You may ask him about himself, but not about others. This is an example of the peculiar code of honor by which our students are guided. Well, the university president has also to get on reasonably well with these other two groups—with students and alumni—who constitute a university, else his tenure of office is likely to be brief.

That reminds me to say something of the tenure of office. It is astonishing how rapidly changes occur in the presidencies of American colleges and universities. I wonder if any of you ever looked the matter up. I did recently because I am completing my twentieth year as president. I have seen changes in the presidencies of Harvard, Yale, Princeton, Pennsylvania, Johns Hopkins, Chicago, Brown, Wesleyan, and all the colleges and universities of New England but two. There is not to-day a president in a college or university to which young men repair in the State of New York who held office when I was appointed, nearly twenty years ago. In the middle west and far west we have state institutions, nearly four dozen of them. Not a single state university has to-day the same president as it had when I was elected to the presidency of Cornell. In the World's Almanac of that time, there were nearly five hundred institutions called colleges and universities. Some four hundred and sixty or seventy have changed presidents in the interval. I begin, Mr. Chancellor, to be retrospective. I shake hands with you, venerable sir (nodding to Henry Bond Elliot), while I congratulate you on the admirable and eloquent speech with which you represented the alumni this morning.

I believe our Bibles tell us that when the sons of God presented themselves, Satan came also. I understand that modern commentators declare that Satan wasn't an evil spirit, but the sifting agency of Providence. We presidents of colleges and universities are in constant contact with that disposition of Providence, and the changes brought about by it are exceedingly numerous. But don't for a moment infer, Mr. Chancellor, because I present these facts, for facts they are, that I don't agree with my friend Butler, that the office is a good one to hold. You will have a man's work to do, two men's work indeed, most of the time. So that the first qualification to-day for a university presidency is good health. And the second, since you are always exposed to criticism, or likely to be, is a tough skin. But there is much work to do, and it is enjoyable work, and it is the best work there is in the world. That is the thing about it that dignifies and exalts the office. We are engaged in a work which everybody recognizes, as, if not the most important work in the world; at any rate second only to that of moral and religious reform. And we have got the public, I believe, more enthusiastically and confidently behind us to-day than any other calling. And we are doing a most important work. And it is a great thing for any university president to be privileged to feel himself a leader in that work, to be the first servant of the university, to represent the scholars and the scientists, who in very truth constitute the university, to be chief adviser, not the only adviser, still less the dictator, but to be the chief adviser in connection with the great work to which the University is dedicated. This, Mr. Chancellor, is the sort of work to which we bid you welcome and in which we wish you God-speed."

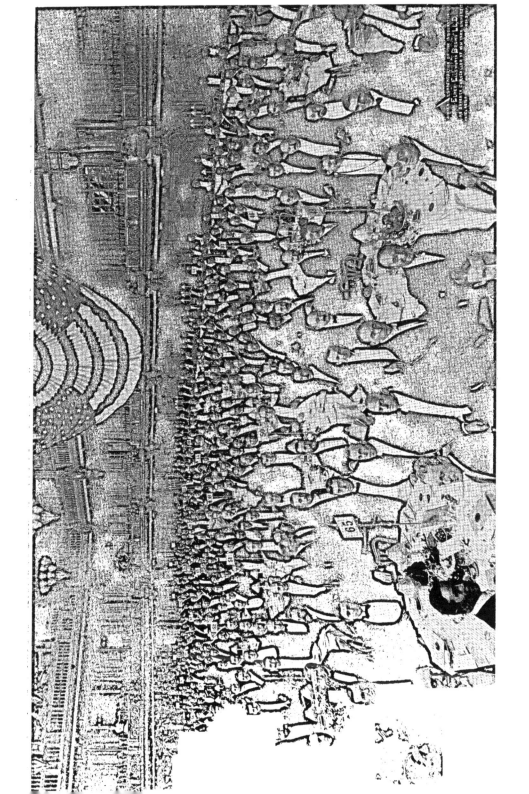

THEODORE FRELINGHUYSEN, LL.D.
1839-1850

JAMES M. MATHEWS, D.D.
1831-1839

ISAAC FERRIS, D.D., LL.D.
1852-1870.

JOHN HALL, D.D., LL.D.,
1881-1891

HOWARD CROSBY, D.D., LL.D.,
1870-1881

LIST OF DELEGATES

FROM INSTITUTIONS IN FOREIGN COUNTRIES

UNIVERSITY OF OXFORD—1
> RT. HON. JAMES BRYCE, O.M., D.C.L., LL.D., D.Litt.,
> British Ambassador; Honorary Fellow of Trinity
> and Oriel Colleges.

UNIVERSITY OF ABERDEEN—2
> ANDREW CARNEGIE, LL.D., Lord Rector.

UNIVERSITY OF CHRISTIANIA—2A
> RAGENWALD INGELSIGTON, M.D., Fellow.

DALHOUSIE COLLEGE—3
> GEORGE W. SCHURMAN, B.A., LL.B., Alumnus.

UNIVERSITY OF TORONTO—4
> HON. Mr. JUSTICE WILLIAM RENWICK RIDDELL,
> L.H.D., F.B.S., Member of the Senate of the Uni-
> versity of Toronto.

McGILL UNIVERSITY—5
> JOHN GODFREY SAXE, ESQ., Alumnus.

ROBERT COLLEGE, TURKEY—6
> REV. EDWARD B. COE, D.D., Trustee.

SYRIAN PROTESTANT COLLEGE—6A
> FREDERICK JONES BLISS, Ph.D., Alumnus.

NANKING UNIVERSITY, CHINA—7
> REV. JOHN WILLIAMS, M.A., D.D., Vice-President.

URUMIA COLLEGE, PERSIA—8
> REV. W. A. SHEDD, D.D., Professor.

MEIJI GAKUIN COLLEGE, JAPAN—9
> J. O. BALLAGH, A.B., Professor.

FROM INSTITUTIONS IN THE UNITED STATES

UNITED STATES BUREAU OF EDUCATION—10
> FLETCHER B. DRESSLAR, Ph.D., Specialist in School
> Hygiene and Sanitation.

NEW YORK STATE EDUCATION DEPARTMENT—11
> ANDREW S. DRAPER, LL.D., Commissioner.
> AUGUSTUS S. DOWNING, M.A., Pd.D., LL.D., First
> Assistant Commissioner.

HARVARD UNIVERSITY—12
> PAUL HENRY HANUS, LL.D., Professor of Education.

YALE UNIVERSITY—13
>   ARTHUR TWINING HADLEY, LL.D., President.

UNIVERSITY OF PENNSYLVANIA—14
>   EDGAR FAHS SMITH, Ph.D., Sc.D., LL.D., Provost.
>   JOSIAH H. PENNIMAN, Ph.D., LL.D., Vice-Provost.

PRINCETON UNIVERSITY—15
>   HENRY BURCHARD FINE, Ph.D., LL.D., Dean of the
>   Faculty; Dean of Departments of Science; Dod
>   Professor of Mathematics.
>   WILLIAM FRANCIS MAGIE, Ph.D., Professor of Physics.

COLUMBIA UNIVERSITY—16
>   NICHOLAS MURRAY BUTLER, Ph.D., Litt.D., LL.D.,
>   President.
>   FREDERICK PAUL KEPPEL, A.B., Dean of the College.

BROWN UNIVERSITY—17
>   ALEXANDER MEIKLEJOHN, Ph.D., Dean.

RUTGERS COLLEGE—18
>   WILLIAM HENRY STEELE DEMAREST, D.D., LL.D.,
>   President.

DARTMOUTH COLLEGE—19
>   ERNEST FOX NICHOLS, Sc.D., LL.D., President.
>   CHARLES F. MATHEWSON, M.A., Trustee.

HAMPDEN SIDNEY COLLEGE—20
>   JUDGE ROGER ATKINSON PRYOR, LL.D., Senior
>   Alumnus.
>   CLEMENT C. GAINES, M.A., Alumnus.

DICKINSON COLLEGE—21
>   EUGENE ALLEN NOBLE, Ph.D., S.T.D., L.H.D., Presi-
>   dent.
>   HORATIO C. KING, A.M., LL.D., Alumnus.

ST. JOHN'S COLLEGE—22
>   THOMAS FELL, Ph.D., D.C.L., LL.D., President.
>   HERBERT NOBLE, LL.D., Alumnus.

UNIVERSITY OF PITTSBURG—23
>   SAMUEL BLACK MCCORMICK, D.D., LL.D., Chancellor.
>   S. B. LINHART, A.M., D.D., Secretary.

GEORGETOWN UNIVERSITY—24
>   JOSEPH HAVENS RICHARDS, S.J., former President.
>   JEAN FELIX POULAIN DES GARENNES, LL.M., Alumnus.

UNIVERSITY OF NORTH CAROLINA—25
>   FRANCIS PRESTON VENABLE, Ph.D., Sc.D., LL.D.,
>   President.
>   AUGUSTUS VAN WYCK, M.A., Alumnus.

UNIVERSITY OF VERMONT—26
> Samuel Eliot Bassett, Ph.D., Professor of Greek.

WILLIAMS COLLEGE—26A
> Asa Hervey Morton, L.H.D., Professor of Natural Theology.

WASHINGTON AND TUSCULUM COLLEGE—27
> C. O. Gray, D.D., President.

BOWDOIN COLLEGE—28
> W. W. Lawrence, Ph.D., Alumnus.

UNIVERSITY OF TENNESSEE—29
> Brown Ayres, Ph.D., D.C.L., LL.D., President.

UNION UNIVERSITY—30
> Charles Alexander Richmond, D.D., Chancellor of Union University; President of Union College.

LIBRARY OF CONGRESS—31
> Herbert Putnam, LL.D., Librarian.

MIDDLEBURY COLLEGE—32
> John Martin Thomas, D.D., President.
> Alonzo Barton Hepburn, D.C.L., LL.D., Trustee.

WASHINGTON AND JEFFERSON COLLEGE—33
> James David Moffat, D.D., LL.D., President.

MIAMI UNIVERSITY—34
> Benjamin Marshall Davis, Ph.D., Professor of Agricultural Education.

THEOLOGICAL SEMINARY OF THE PRESBYTERIAN CHURCH AT PRINCETON, N. J.—35
> James Oscar Boyd, Ph.D., Professor of Old Testament Literature.

HAMILTON COLLEGE—36
> Elihu Root, LL.D., Chairman of the Board of Trustees.

GENERAL THEOLOGICAL SEMINARY—37
> Herbert McKenzie Denslow, D.D., Acting Dean.
> Rev. Charles N. Shepard, M.A., B.D., Professor.

AUBURN THEOLOGICAL SEMINARY—38
> George Black Stewart, D.D., LL.D., President.

UNIVERSITY OF VIRGINIA—39
> Charles Baskerville, Ph.D., F.C.S., Alumnus.
> Robert L. Harrison, Esq., Alumnus.

COLGATE UNIVERSITY—40
> William Magnum Lawrence, D.D., President of the Corporation.

NORWICH UNIVERSITY—41
> Edward D. Adams, LL.D., Alumnus.
> Charles H. Nichols, C.E., Alumnus.

AMHERST COLLEGE—42
>George Harris, D.D., LL.D., President.
>Frederic Lincoln Thompson, M.A., Professor of History.

GEORGE WASHINGTON UNIVERSITY—43
>Charles H. Stockton, LL.D., President.

TRINITY COLLEGE (CONN.)—44
>Henry Augustus Perkins, E.E., M.A., Professor of Physics.

KENYON COLLEGE—45
>John Brooks Leavitt, LL.D., Alumnus.

RENSSELAER POLYTECHNIC INSTITUTE—46
>Palmer Chamberlaine Ricketts, C.E., E.D., LL.D., President.
>Dwinel French Thompson, B.S., Professor of Descriptive Geometry.

THEOLOGICAL SEMINARY OF THE REFORMED CHURCH IN THE UNITED STATES—47
>John Preston Searle, D.D., President.

WESTERN RESERVE UNIVERSITY—48
>Charles Francis Thwing, S.T.D., LL.D., President.

ILLINOIS COLLEGE—49
>Thomas W. Smith, D.D., Trustee.

RANDOLPH-MACON COLLEGE—50
>Robert Emery Blackwell, M.A., President.

WESLEYAN UNIVERSITY—51
>William Arnold Shanklin, L.H.D., D.D., LL.D., President.

LAFAYETTE COLLEGE—52
>Ethelbert Dudley Warfield, D.D., LL.D., President.

PENNSYLVANIA COLLEGE—53
>William Anthony Granville, Ph.D., President.
>Junius Benjamin Remensnyder, D.D., LL.D., Alumnus.

HAVERFORD COLLEGE—54
>Isaac Sharpless, Sc.D., L.H.D., LL.D., President.

OBERLIN COLLEGE—55
>Charles Whiting Williams, M.A., Assistant to the President.

HARTFORD THEOLOGICAL SEMINARY—56
>Lewis Bayles Paton, D.D., LL.D., Nettleton Professor of Old Testament Exegesis and Criticism.
>Edwin Knox Mitchell, D.D., Professor.

TULANE UNIVERSITY—57
>F. H. Kohlman, LL.B., President New York Alumni Association.

UNION THEOLOGICAL SEMINARY—58
> Francis Brown, Ph.D., Litt.D., D.D., LL.D., President.
> Charles Ripley Gillett, D.D., L.H.D., Secretary to the Faculty.

ALFRED UNIVERSITY—59
> Boothe Colwell Davis, Ph.D., President.

UNIVERSITY OF LOUISVILLE—60
> John Patterson, M.A., Litt.M., LL.D., Dean of College of Arts and Sciences.

KNOX COLLEGE—61
> Thomas McClelland, D.D., LL.D., President.

UNIVERSITY OF MICHIGAN—62
> Harry Burns Hutchins, LL.D., President.

MOUNT HOLYOKE COLLEGE—63
> Mary Emma Woolley, L.H.D., President.
> Clayton Charles Kohl, Ph.D., Professor of Education.

DE PAUW UNIVERSITY—63A
> Guy M. Walker, Esq., Alumnus.

TRINITY COLLEGE (N. C.)—64
> William Preston Few, LL.D., President.

FORDHAM UNIVERSITY—65
> V. E. Sorapure, M.B., Ch.B., F.R.C.S., Pro-Dean of the Schools of Medicine and Pharmacy.

UNIVERSITY OF MISSOURI—66
> Walter Rautenstrauch, B.S., Alumnus.

BELOIT COLLEGE—67
> Edward Dwight Eaton, D.D., LL.D., President.

CARROLL COLLEGE—67A
> Charles L. Thompson, D.D., LL.D., Alumnus.

SMITHSONIAN INSTITUTION—68
> Frederick W. True, M.S., LL.D., Assistant Secretary.

EARLHAM COLLEGE—69
> Samuel B. Heckman, Ph.D., Alumnus.
> Robert Underwood Johnson, L.H.D., Alumnus.

STATE UNIVERSITY OF IOWA—70
> William B. Guthrie, Ph.D., Alumnus.

COLLEGE OF THE CITY OF NEW YORK—71
> John Huston Finley, A.M., LL.D., President.
> Fitz Gerald Tisdall, Ph.D., Professor of the Greek Language and Literature.
> Harry C. Krowl, Ph.D., Assistant Professor of English.

Louis Delamarre, Ph.D., Assistant Professor of French.

Charles A. Downer, Ph.D., Professor of Romance Languages.

GRINNELL COLLEGE—72
Joseph Hanson Thomas Main, Ph.D., President.
Albert Shaw, Ph.D., LL.D., Alumnus.

ST. FRANCIS XAVIER COLLEGE—73
Joseph H. Rockwell, S.J., President.

UNIVERSITY OF WISCONSIN—74
Gilbert E. Roe, Esq., Alumnus.
Walter T. Arndt, A.M., Alumnus.

UNIVERSITY OF ROCHESTER—75
Frederick Jones Bliss, Ph.D., Dean.

NORTHWESTERN UNIVERSITY—76
Abram Winegartner Harris, Sc.D., LL.D., President.
Milo Roy Maltbie, Ph.D., Alumnus.
Arlo Ayres Brown, A.B., Alumnus.

TUFTS COLLEGE—77
Frank George Wren, A.M., Dean of Faculty of Arts and Sciences and Faculty of College of Letters.

CORNELL COLLEGE—78
Edward T. Divine, Ph.D., LL.D., Alumnus.

BROOKLYN POLYTECHNIC INSTITUTE—79
Fred Washington Atkinson, Ph.D., President.

PENNSYLVANIA STATE COLLEGE—80
Addams Stratton McAllister, E.E., Ph.D., Professorial Lecturer in Electrical Engineering.

LENOX COLLEGE—80A
Elmer Ellsworth Reed, D.D., President.

ST. STEPHENS COLLEGE—81
William C. Rodgers, M.A., S.T.O., President.

ST. LAWRENCE UNIVERSITY—81A
Almon Gunnison, D.D., LL.D., President.

ALBION COLLEGE—82
Samuel Dickie, M.S., LL.D., President.
Frank Andrews Fall, M.A., Alumnus.

MASSACHUSETTS INSTITUTE OF TECHNOLOGY —83
George B. Wendell, Ph.D., Alumnus.
Charles Russell Richards, M.E., Alumnus.

VASSAR COLLEGE—84
James Monroe Taylor, D.D., LL.D., President.
Lucy Maynard Salmon, M.A., Professor of History.
Daniel Smiley, Trustee.

KANSAS STATE AGRICULTURAL COLLEGE—85
PAUL H. FAIRCHILD, M.D., Alumnus.

MANHATTAN COLLEGE—86
BROTHER POTAMIAN, Sc.D.

UNIVERSITY OF WASHINGTON—87
CHARLES CHURCH MORE, C.E., M.S., Associate Professor of Civil Engineering.

BATES COLLEGE—88
GEORGE COLBY CHASE, D.D., LL.D., President.
WILLIS EUGENE LOUGEE, M.A., Alumnus.
ALBERT FIELDS GILMORE, B.A., Alumnus.

GALLAUDET COLLEGE—89
EDWARD ALLEN FAY, Ph.D., Vice-President.

MASSACHUSETTS AGRICULTURAL COLLEGE—90
KENYON LEECH BUTTERFIELD, M.A., President.
GEORGE F. MILLS, B.S., Dean.

UNIVERSITY OF KANSAS—91
EDWIN EMERY SLOSSON, Ph.D., Alumnus.

UNIVERSITY OF MAINE—92
ALLEN ROGERS, Ph.D., Alumnus.
JEREMIAH SWEETSER FERGUSON, M.S., M.D., Alumnus.

WORCESTER POLYTECHNIC INSTITUTE—93
ALEXANDER WILMER DUFF, Sc.D., Professor of Physics.

LEHIGH UNIVERSITY—94
NATT M. EMERY, M.A., Vice-President.
CHARLES L. THORNBURG, C.E. Ph.D., Professor of Mathematics and Astronomy.

UNIVERSITY OF WOOSTER—94A
LOUIS H. SEVERANCE, ESQ., President Board of Trustees.

DREW THEOLOGICAL SEMINARY—95
ROBERT WILLIAM ROGERS, Ph.D., Litt.D., D.D., LL.D., Professor of Hebrew and Old Testament Exegesis.

CORNELL UNIVERSITY—96
JACOB GOULD SCHURMAN, Sc.D., LL.D., President.

HOWARD UNIVERSITY—97
WILBUR PATTERSON THIRKIELD, D.D., LL.D., President.

MUHLENBERG COLLEGE—98
JOHN A. W. HAAS, D.D., President.
GEORGE T. ETTINGER, Ph.D., Dean.

UNIVERSITY OF ILLINOIS—99
EDMUND JANES JAMES, Ph.D., LL.D., President.

OLIVET COLLEGE—100
GEORGE CLARE SPRAGUE, Ph.D., Alumnus.

UNIVERSITY OF CALIFORNIA—101
HARRY ALLEN OVERSTREET, A.B., Alumnus.

UNIVERSITY OF MINNESOTA—102
CHARLES PETER BERKEY, Ph.D., Alumnus.

WELLS COLLEGE—103
GEORGE MORGAN WARD, D.D., LL.D., President.
LOUIS FRANKLIN SNOW, Ph.D., Professor of Education.

BOSTON UNIVERSITY—104
LEMUEL HERBERT MURLIN, D.D., LL.D., President.
MARCUS DARIUS BUELL, D.D., Dean.

PURDUE UNIVERSITY—105
DANIEL RALPH LUCAS, Ph.D., M.D., Alumnus.

SWARTHMORE COLLEGE—106
JOSEPH SWAIN, LL.D., President.
ISAAC H. CLOTHIER, M.A., Trustee.

URSINUS COLLEGE—107
ALBERT EDWARD KEIGWIN, D.D., President.
GEORGE LESLIE OMWAKE, Ph.D.

UNIVERSITY OF ARKANSAS—108
JOHN NEWTON TILLMAN, LL.D., President.

NORMAL COLLEGE OF THE CITY OF NEW YORK
—109
GEORGE SAMLER DAVIS, LL.D., President.
EDWARD S. BURGESS, Ph.D., Sc.D., Professor of Natural Science.

OHIO STATE UNIVERSITY—110
WILLIAM OXLEY THOMPSON, D.D., LL.D., President.
HALBERT E. PAYNE, A.B., Alumnus.
RALPH D. MERSHON, C.E., Alumnus.

METROPOLITAN MUSEUM OF ART—111
EDWARD ROBINSON, LL.D., Director.

STEVENS INSTITUTE OF TECHNOLOGY—112
ALEXANDER CROMBIE HUMPHREYS, LL.D., President.

SMITH COLLEGE—113
MARION LE ROY BURTON, Ph.D., D.D., President.

VANDERBILT UNIVERSITY—114
JAMES HAMPTON KIRKLAND, Ph.D., D.C.L., LL.D.,
President.

THE CHAUTAUQUA INSTITUTION—115
FRANK CHAPIN BRAY, Ph.B., Editor.

COLORADO COLLEGE—116
WILLIAM FREDERICK SLOCUM, D.D., LL.D., President.

PARK COLLEGE—117
REV. JOHN L. CAUGHEY, D.D., Alumnus.

WELLESLEY COLLEGE—118
SARAH FRANCES WHITING, Sc.D., Professor of Physics
and Director of the Whitin Observatory.

PARSONS COLLEGE—119
PHILO C. HILDRETH, M.A., Professor.

JOHNS HOPKINS UNIVERSITY—120
GEORGE DRAYTON STRAYER, Ph.D., Alumnus.

LAKE FOREST COLLEGE—121
ROBERT ALMER HARPER, Ph.D.

THE SOUTHERN EDUCATION BOARD—121A
ROBERT C. OGDEN, M.A., LL.D., President.

UNIVERSITY OF TEXAS—122
JOSEPH LINDSEY HENDERSON, M.A., Associate Professor of Secondary Education.

COE COLLEGE—123
CHARLES M. JESUP, ESQ., Trustee.

BRYN MAWR COLLEGE—124
M. CAREY THOMAS, Ph.D., LL.D., President
MARY E. GARRETT, Member of Board of Directors.

CASE SCHOOL OF APPLIED SCIENCE—125
CHARLES SUMNER HOWE, Ph.D., Sc.D., LL.D., President.

UNIVERSITY OF SOUTH DAKOTA—126
ARNOLD L. DAVIS, A.B., Alumnus.

UNIVERSITY OF NORTH DAKOTA—126A
MAXWELL M. UPSON, A.B., M.E., Alumnus.

GOUCHER COLLEGE—127
JOHN B. VAN METER, LL.D., Acting President.
MRS. WILLIAM VAN VALZAH HAYES, A.B., Alumnus.

LELAND STANFORD JUNIOR UNIVERSITY—128
DAVID SAMUEL SNEDDEN, Ph.D., Alumnus.

JEWISH THEOLOGICAL SEMINARY—129
SOLOMON SCHECHTER, Litt.D., President.

AMERICAN MUSEUM OF NATURAL HISTORY—130
FREDERIC A. LUCAS, Sc.D., Director.

OCCIDENTAL COLLEGE—131
W. R. CRANE, A.B., Alumnus.

CLARK UNIVERSITY—132
HENRY TABER, Ph.D., Professor of Mathematics.

UNIVERSITY OF CHICAGO—133
HARRY PRATT JUDSON, M.A., LL.D., President.

UNIVERSITY OF ARIZONA—134
EDWIN M. BLAKE, ESQ., Alumnus.

THE CHICAGO TRAINING SCHOOL AND INSTI-
TUTE—135
ISAAC EDDY BROWN, A.M.

MILLS COLLEGE—136
MRS. PHILIP CARPENTER, A.B., Alumnus.

POMONA COLLEGE—137
ALFRED CUMMINGS REED, M.D., Alumnus.

ADELPHI COLLEGE—138
CHARLES HERBERT LEVERMORE, Ph.D., President.
WILLIAM CLARK PECKHAM, M.A., Dean and Professor
of Physics.

THE CARNEGIE TECHNICAL SCHOOLS—139
ARTHUR ARTON HAMERSCHLAG, Sc.D., Director.

CLARK COLLEGE—140
EDMUND CLARK SANFORD, Ph.D., Sc.D., President.
MARTIN ANDREE ROSANOFF, Sc.D., Assistant Professor
of Chemistry.

ROCKEFELLER INSTITUTE FOR MEDICAL RE-
SEARCH—141
JEROME D. GREENE, A.B., General Manager.

CARNEGIE INSTITUTION OF WASHINGTON—142
ELIHU ROOT, LL.D., Trustee

GENERAL EDUCATION BOARD—143
STARR J. MURPHY, A.B., LL.B., Member of the Board.

CARNEGIE FOUNDATION FOR THE ADVANCE-
MENT OF TEACHING—144
HENRY SMITH PRITCHETT, Sc.D., Ph.D., LL.D., Presi-
dent.
ABRAHAM FLEXNER, M.A.

RUSSELL SAGE FOUNDATION—145
JOHN MARK GLENN, LL.B., M.A., Director.
LEONARD P. AYRES, Ph.D., Associate Director of the
Department of Child Hygiene.

DOMINION OF CANADA ROYAL COMMISSION ON
TECHNICAL EDUCATION—146
JAMES W. ROBERTSON, C.M.G., D.Sc., LL.D., Chairman.
GEORGE BRYCE, D.Sc.

AMERICAN SCANDINAVIAN SOCIETY—147
CARL LORENTZEN, Secretary.

INAUGURATION COMMITTEES

GENERAL INAUGURATION COMMITTEE

William M. Kingsley, A.M., *Chairman*.
Lyman Abbott, D.D., LL.D., L.H.D.
Clarence D. Ashley, J.D., LL.D.
J. Edgar Bull, A.B., LL.B.
William F. Havemeyer.
Willis Fletcher Johnson, L.H.D.
Clarence Hill Kelsey, A.B., LL.B., A.M.
Egbert Le Fevre, M.D., Sc.D., LL.D.
John H. MacCracken, Ph.D.
William S. Opdyke, A.B.
James A. O'Gorman, LL.D.
Elihu Root, LL.D.
Isaac F. Russell, D.C.L., J.D., LL.D.
Eugene Stevenson, A.B.
John J. Stevenson, Ph.D., LL.D.
Francis H. Stoddard, Ph.D.
George A. Strong, A.B., LL.B.

DIRECTOR OF CEREMONIES
Edward Hagaman Hall, L.H.M., L.H.D.

CHAIRMEN OF COMMITTEES

Chronicler................Ernest Gottlieb Sihler, Ph.D.
Coat and Robing Room..........Arthur H. Nason, A.M.
Decoration......................Collins P. Bliss, A.M.
Dinner.............................James Abbott, A.B.
Finance....................William M. Kingsley, A.M.
Invitation........................Frank A. Fall, A.M.
Luncheon...................Archibald T. Bouton, A.M.
Grand Marshal................George C. Sprague, Ph.D.
Medical College................Samuel A. Brown, M.D.
Program...............Elmer E. Brown, Ph.D., LL.D.
Reception...................John H. MacCracken, Ph.D.
Registration Bureau..............Arthur B. Lamb, Ph.D.
Undergraduates....................Thomas J. Crawford
Ushers..................Thomas W. Edmondson, Ph.D.
Washington Square........Joseph French Johnson, D.C.S.

Lightning Source UK Ltd.
Milton Keynes UK
UKHW010009090219
336872UK00005B/136/P